LATTER-DAY SAINT

# Heroes & Heroines

TRUE STORIES OF COURAGE & FAITH

Marlene Bateman Sullivan

# LATTER-DAY SAINT Heroes & Heroines

## TRUE STORIES OF COURAGE & FAITH

Marlene Bateman Sullivan

Salt Lake City, Utah

LDS Heroes and Heroines:



Library of Congress Cataloging-in-Publication Data
Sullivan, Marlene Bateman
Latter-day Saint heroes and heroines : true stories of courage and faith / Marlene
Bateman Sullivan
p. cm.
Includes index, bibliographical references.
ISBN 1-56236-242-9
1. Mormons—Biography. I. Title.
BX8693.S85 1999
289.3'092'2—dc21 99-37731
[B] CIP

Printed in the United States of America

Cover art: *Nauvoo Farewell: The Exodus Begins* and
all interior art by Frank M. Thomas. Used by permission.

*To Mark, a different kind of hero*

# Table of Contents

LATTER-DAY SAINT

# Heroes & Heroines

TRUE STORIES OF COURAGE & FAITH

# 1

## "It Will Not Do for Me to Die"

### Brother Collins

Driven from their homes during the cold winter of 1846, the Saints gathered to camp on the banks of the Missouri River. Because of hardships imposed by the lack of food, frigid weather, and inadequate living conditions, people began suffering from a variety of illnesses that spread quickly through the encampment. Brother Collins was among those who became sick, soon becoming seriously ill. Though not a member of the Church, he was with the Saints because his wife was a devout member, and he had followed after the Mormons as they were driven from place to place.

Brother Collins's health rapidly deteriorated until he began drifting in and out of consciousness. For many days, he lay nearly comatose, and friends felt that he would not recover. However, one morning Elder A. O. Smoot was sitting beside his bed keeping watch when the invalid's eyes flickered open.

Surprised at signs of life, Elder Smoot asked, "Do you have any message to give before dying?"

"It will not do for me to die yet," Brother Collins murmured stoutly, "as I have not yet been baptized. I want you to take me to the river, now, and perform this ordinance."

Shocked at the idea of taking such a seriously ill man outside in the dead of winter, Elder Smoot protested. But Brother Collins was so insistent that he finally promised to discuss the matter with the men in camp. The brethren decided that it was only proper to grant the last wish of a dying man, although they were more than a little hesitant to take such a debilitated person out in such weather, much less immerse him in icy water.

Once they informed Brother Collins they would do as he wished, there was the problem of getting the bedridden man to the river. They picked up Brother Collins's bed with his weakened form still on it and carried it outside where they set it upon a large board, then transported board, bed, and man to a waiting wagon.

On the way to the river, the metal strip around the wagon's wheel started to come off and the elders had to stop to repair it. As they were hammering, Brother Collins's weak but penetrating voice called out from inside the wagon, asking what had happened.

Upon hearing that the wheel had to be fixed, he hollered back, "Oh never mind the tire! Go on, or I'll die and go to hell before I'm baptized!"

The men hurried with their repairs and soon continued their journey. Finally, they reached the river, which was completely frozen over except for small areas near the shore. Great chunks of ice had been cut out so that the camp could draw water and the animals could drink.

Gently, the men lifted Brother Collins from the wagon and carried him into the frigid water. Shivering with cold, Elder Smoot baptized Brother Collins and pronounced a blessing upon him, promising that his health would be restored. Then the men lifted the invalid out of the water, quickly wrapped a blanket around him, and left him to sit on a block of ice on the shore. One man sat with him while the others went to the wagon.

ETHOMAS

"Where are they going?" Brother Collins asked curiously.

"They're going to turn it around and bring your bed here so we can carry you back to the wagon and take you home."

"Oh, you don't need to go to all that trouble," Brother Collins replied calmly. "I can walk back easily enough."

To the astonishment of the brethren, Brother Collins did walk back, and it was not long before he completely regained his good health.

# 2

# She Watched Her House Burn

## The Unwavering Convert

In 1885, Elder Edward J. Wood was on a mission in the Samoan Islands when he was asked by a Latter-day Saint couple to accompany them on a visit to their parents. He agreed and went with them to a nearby island. However, the parents were not well pleased to have Elder Wood as a guest. The father was a teacher in another religion and hostile toward the Mormons. Meanwhile, word circulated through the village that a "Mamona" had arrived, and Elder Wood was asked to hold a meeting.

Although his hosts, the couple's parents, were against it, their children encouraged Elder Wood to hold a meeting that very evening. Most of the village—several hundred people—attended out of curiosity to listen to the missionary preach about the latter-day restoration of the Church of Jesus Christ. Elder Wood wrote about the evening. "A very exceptional spirit for good was felt." After the meeting, they all filed out except for one couple and their parents. The lady of the one couple said she was deeply impressed with the glad news of the 'Old Church' being revealed anew to the Earth in our day and she wanted another meeting the next afternoon." Little did Elder Wood know of the dire consequences this woman would suffer as a result of his preaching.

An even larger crowd gathered at the next meeting. But the feelings of the people had undergone a change, mostly due to the unfriendly attitude of the couple's parents. Before this, the people had been respectfully curious and even friendly, but now there were dark mutterings, and the people seemed full of animosity.

At the close of the meeting, the council of chiefs approached Elder Wood and told him to leave the island immediately. The woman who had asked Elder Wood to hold the meeting then joined the conversation. Elder Wood stated, "With a fine humble spirit she told him [the spokesman] she was ready to be baptized and become a Mamona."

The chiefs were angry at this display of support for a preacher whom they had just banished. Turning away abruptly, they left without another word.

The woman then asked Elder Wood if he had the authority to baptize her. She told him she had been converted the first time she had heard him speak. Elder Wood replied that he did have the authority but that it was important for her to obtain the consent of her husband. Her husband, who had been standing nearby, voiced his opinion that her baptism would be unwise. He realized that the chiefs' touchy pride had been wounded but said that she could do as she wished.

While the couple talked with Elder Wood, the chiefs, furious at the woman's disregard of their authority, decided to react quickly and harshly.

Elder Wood relates, "While we were talking, the council of chiefs sent word that if this woman joined our church, her house and all the belongings would be burned to the ground." Soberly, the new convert considered the warning, but already her faith was too strong to allow her to back away from what she recognized as the truth. Elder Wood continued, "This edict only made the good woman all the more anxious to be baptized and said she would be ready to be baptized that night when the tide would be in."

News quickly spread through the village that one of the islanders had been converted to this "new" religion and was going to be baptized that very night. That evening, the new convert wore a beautiful white dress and after gathering her family around her, asked the missionary to follow them to the stream.

"She walked with the dignity and bearing of a chieftess," Elder Wood said later. "The entire village lined the walk through the beautiful palms to the water's edge. It was a glorious moonlit night and it appeared that through the trees the light of heaven was present."

When she reached the water, the natives gathered around respectfully and sang a haunting melody. The spirit was very strong, and while the others watched silently, Elder Wood baptized the woman. Then, on the water's edge, she knelt during her confirmation.

After the "amen," the beautiful peace of the evening was suddenly broken as some members of the crowd let out wild shrieks before racing off into the woods. The woman and her family ran off also.

With a sinking heart, Elder Wood followed, fearing the worst, yet hoping that after such a stirring baptism the chiefs would not go through with their threats. His heart was pounding when finally he reached the village. A group of men was hurrying from home to home, asking people to come and help burn the house of the "Mamona" woman.

He found the newly baptized sister standing with her family in front of her home. The chiefs appeared, their stern faces glistening with sweat in the light of the torches. They demanded that she renounce her new religion and threatened that if she did not, they would command the torch be set to her home. The glowing light of the full moon illuminated the woman, brightening the whiteness of her dress to an unearthly radiance, setting her apart from the others.

Elder Wood said of that moment, "She stood erect before all of them and in the light of the moon, bore one of the most sincere testimonies of the divinity of the 'New' church and of my mission among them, and prophesied that every chief that was in favor of burning her home would soon die an unnatural death."

The haughty chiefs remained untouched by her solemn and stirring testimony and angrily demanded that blazing torches be set to the dwelling. Flames ran around the home, shooting up the sides and quickly engulfing it in a fiery inferno. There was no time to retrieve any belongings and the family wept, brokenhearted, as their home burned to the ground.

Elder Wood felt sick as he watched the house go up in a fiery blaze and worried about the safety of his new convert. The woman, sensitive to his feelings, came over to reassure and comfort him. Over and over, she told him not to be sad, repeating it loudly enough so that all could hear. Later, friends took the family in for the night.

The next morning, the woman came over and asked Elder Wood if he would take her to a nearby island where her father, a powerful head chief, lived. After greeting her father, they sat on mats while she told him all that had happened. He listened intently to the full story, then called a council with his chiefs. After their meeting, he asked Elder Wood to take him and his daughter back to her island.

Their arrival set off a ripple of surprise and alarm. The people were subdued at having such an important

F. THOMAS 1999

chief on their island, especially after the events of the previous night. Reverently, they bowed to their distinguished visitor as he went straight to the local chiefs and asked if they would walk with him and the "Mamona" elder through the village. Quietly, they agreed. After strolling for a few minutes, the head chief stopped in a clearing and turned to Elder Wood.

"To my great surprise, he asked me to select a site where I would like to have a church house and a dwelling house. He then turned to the Chiefs who had burned his daughter's house and told them that he and his council had decided that they had to build me a house and a house for a church on any site I chose." In six weeks, Elder Wood had a new home and a meeting house constructed from split bamboo.

"I held meetings and made many converts. We had a very fine branch organized and the whole village became our friends." Although many shared their testimonies within its walls, no one was more steadfast than the woman who had sacrificed her home for the gospel.

Four years later, Elder Wood returned to the island just in time to attend the funeral service of one of the chiefs who had taken part in burning the home of the unwavering convert. He had been the last survivor, as all the others had preceded him in death.

# 3

## Baptism in Icy Waters

Jane Snyder

Although Jane Snyder was an easy-going person, she was not one to let people push her around. She firmly resisted the efforts of her older brother Robert to baptize her, though the rest of her family had been baptized Christians long ago. Jane didn't object to the doctrine that said a person had to be baptized to receive a remission of sins, but felt that because *she* had no sins to repent of, there was no need for the cleansing ordinance of baptism.

Jane was born in January of 1823, in Pamela, New York, the tenth of eleven children. Her father, Isaac Snyder, was a well-to-do farmer of no religious preference. Her mother, Lovisa, was a devout Methodist. The family later moved to Ontario, Canada.

Robert became ill and for nearly three years suffered with tuberculosis. During that time, he studied the scriptures intensely, becoming convinced that baptism by immersion was the only proper method of baptism. He continued praying for truth and guidance, asking for someone who could properly perform this ordinance. One night, during fervent prayer, he heard a quiet voice whisper a name—John E. Page—and began a search to find this man, but to no avail.

A few weeks later, Mormon missionaries came to the area and held a meeting within two miles of the Snyder home. Many were converted during the meeting, one of them being Jane's married sister, who kept the news secret from her family—that is, until someone knocked on their door to inform Mr. and Mrs. Snyder that their daughter Sarah had been baptized. The parents were embarrassed, while Robert's reaction was one of jubilant shock when he found that the name of one of the missionaries was Page.

Robert then told his parents about his prayer and conviction about proper baptism. He insisted on meeting with the missionaries to confirm that the elder who had baptized his sister was indeed John E. Page. It was, in fact, so, and Elder Page and his companion taught the whole family the gospel. They anointed and blessed Robert, which greatly improved his health. He was baptized the following April, then himself went on a mission, baptizing many. These included all his family, except for Jane and two brothers.

When Church leaders counseled members to gather in Missouri, the Snyders began the journey but had to stop in La Porte, Indiana, when Jane's little niece became too ill to travel. While there, the family received word that the Prophet Joseph Smith wanted them to remain in Indiana for a few years to provide a place for missionaries to stay.

Always a frail person, Jane became seriously ill herself and was soon bedridden, suffering extreme pain. After three weeks, her condition worsened until she was unable to move or even speak. When Robert returned for a visit, he found Jane paralyzed and close to death.

As she recounted later, "At this time my brother Robert had fasted for days on my account. He asked me if he could lay his hands on me and pray for me. I could not speak, but nodded to him. He did so. I could then see for the first time that he had received the gospel of the Lord Jesus and that God had blessed him with the gift of healing. I could then see it was my duty to be baptized."

Robert was still sitting by her bed when Jane lifted one of her arms and whispered that she wanted to be baptized. Her brother told her to wait, as it was midwinter and he feared the exposure might prove fatal. But Jane would not be denied and said she was not afraid of death, only of dying without being baptized.

Looking down on his pale and weak sister, Robert counseled her to wait until she was stronger. Still Jane refused to put it off, fearing not death itself, but death without having the ordinance of baptism performed. All Robert's arguments were in vain, and finally he and his parents gave in to her wishes.

It was a bitterly cold day in January of 1840 when Robert carried a blanket-wrapped Jane to the edge of the frigid river. Word had spread among the community that a Mormon intended on dousing his critically ill sister in the freezing water and nearly three hundred outraged peopled gathered to watch and protest. It took some time for Robert and family members to break a hole through the ice, which was nearly a foot thick. The people shouted angrily and hurled abuses at him, horrified that he would immerse his invalid sister in the chilly water. Some even threatened to arrest him if he continued with his plans.

Jane spoke up. "I want to say to all you people who have come out to see me baptized, that I do it of my own free will and choice, and if you interfere with the man who has baptized me, God will interfere with you."

Robert walked into the freezing water, followed by his brother George who was carrying Jane. Easing her into the river, Robert quickly baptized her. People were still noisily distraught when Jane came up out of the water.

"When I came out, the Spirit of the Lord rested upon me and I spoke to those present and told them that I was now well, I was not cold and if they arrested my brother God would visit them in judgment. I never went to bed any more. I was well from that time and I told them that I had done all this because God had made it known to me by His Spirit that it was my duty and they all left and went home."

This strong outburst surprised everyone who knew Jane, for she was normally a quiet, shy person. The immersion into the icy river had no ill effects on Jane's health but instead seemed to heal her. Free from the illness she had suffered all winter, Jane continued to be valiant and faithful in the coming years.

# 4

# A Weak Heart

Anna Berg

It was an unusual question. What did the temperature of the baptismal water matter? But to Anna Berg, an investigator who had just decided to be baptized, it was a matter of life and death. In response to Anna's question, the elder replied that he didn't know the exact temperature, only that the water would be comfortably warm.

Anna's decision to join the Church was the result of a chance visit from two Mormon missionaries and months of study and prayer. Elder Donald Kristofferson and Elder Calvin Broadhead were tracting in Bergen, Norway. They were carrying a map so they wouldn't miss any homes when they happened upon a house not on the street they were tracting. Because the missionaries were covering each individual street methodically, they debated whether to approach the house or not. As it was close, however, they decided to knock on the door.

When Anna Berg opened the door and saw the shivering missionaries, she kindly invited them in to warm themselves by the fire. But she warned them with a laugh, "I want you to know I don't believe in your church." Famous last words!

They had an enjoyable visit, as she was an avid Bible scholar with a quick mind. Thereafter, the elders came frequently to teach her the lessons, and she contributed as much information in each discussion as they did. Sister Berg's knowledge of the Bible had prepared her to receive the message of the restored gospel, and she was wholly devoted to finding out the truth. At first, she stumbled over the fact that Heavenly Father and Jesus Christ had actually shown themselves to a young boy. The missionaries advised her to pray and ask Heavenly Father to reveal the truth. She did this and felt a strong confirmation of the gospel's restoration through the Prophet Joseph Smith. Soon, she was spreading the news of the gospel to her friends. Anna was close to having a full testimony of the restored gospel when the elders were transferred to a new location. Unable to commit herself unequivocally at that point, she put off baptism.

Elder Kristofferson continued his work in a new area and months passed. Soon, his time in the mission field was almost up. A few days before he was scheduled to return home, he stopped in Bergen and, together with a local elder, went to visit Sister Berg. Tearfully, they were reunited. When Anna begged Elder Kristofferson to stay in the city just a few more days, he replied, "Fru Berg, I'm due in Oslo tomorrow. Only one thing could make it possible for me to stay beyond today."

Anna hesitated, aware that he was referring to her baptism but knowing that he was not aware of the story behind her hesitation. Then came her strange question about the temperature of the baptismal water. She finally confided to him the reason for her delay in joining the Church. Although Anna did have a testimony of the gospel, she was terribly afraid of being baptized because she had a severe heart condition that made her susceptible to sudden shocks and chills. She had a tremendous fear that immersion in baptismal waters could prove fatal for her. Reassured when the missionary told her the water would be pleasantly warm, Anna finally agreed to be baptized.

Elder Kristofferson went to the chapel hours beforehand to make sure everything was ready. The church was on the second floor of a three-story building. The bottom floor held shops, while the top floor housed the missionaries. Under the floorboards of the chapel was the baptismal font. When a section of flooring behind the podium was removed, the stairs that led down into the font were revealed. A nearby heater kept the water warm.

The elder knelt beside the font which had been filled and felt the water to make sure it was warm, then yanked his hand away. The water was icy cold! Elder Kristofferson checked the water heater. Broken! The only thing he could think of doing was to heat water in the missionary's kitchen and rush it downstairs to the font. Other elders helped him transport hot water to warm the chilly baptismal waters.

During this race against time, Elder Kristofferson questioned whether they would be able to heat the water in such a short time. If they could not, would Sister Berg be able to conquer her fear of baptism enough to try again at a later time? The elder was well aware that her love and trust in him played a significant part in overcoming her great fear of being immersed in water. If he went home without baptizing her, would Anna ever dredge up the courage to go through with this important ordinance? Finally, after countless trips, the exhausted elders had carried enough hot water to make the baptismal water feel more comfortable.

A few minutes before the service started, Elder Kristofferson tested the water. It was icy cold again! The pots and pans full of heated water had not been enough to change the temperature for long. The missionary prayed fervently, feeling a grave responsibility for Anna Berg's physical and spiritual well-being. Asking the Lord for direction, Elder Kristofferson felt impressed to go ahead with the ordinance. He felt the Lord would be with her and protect her from any ill effects the cold water might have upon her weak heart.

However, Anna had more than a physically weak heart to overcome. When she had confessed her physical disability to Elder Kristofferson, she did not tell him of another dilemma, one that had its roots in an event that happened long ago. Years before, she had reached the conclusion that infant baptism was not necessary in the sight of the Lord, though she herself had been baptized as an infant. After much studying, Anna began searching for a church that believed in baptism at a later age. She found one and rushed into baptism without taking time to thoroughly study their beliefs. Afterwards, to her acute disappointment, she found that she disagreed with many of the teachings of her new church.

Anna blamed herself for this terrible mistake, feeling that she had relied too much on her reasoning and had not followed the Spirit of the Lord. She believed if she had listened to God, He would not have let her make such a mistake. Anna made a vow never to rely on her own reasoning again but to trust the Lord and his promptings.

Then came the Mormon elders, and Anna felt that they spoke the truth. She believed that the whispering of the Spirit within her was inspiration from the Lord. Yet, she wanted to be completely sure, positive without a doubt. Anna prayed frequently for more than just faith. She prayed for a firm knowledge and told Heavenly Father that she was willing to give up her mortal life to know the truth. Yet she received no spiritual witness, even after agreeing to be baptized. She spent the night before her scheduled baptism in prayer, but still there was no answer.

The long morning passed, and Anna felt restless and confused, waiting for an answer to her prayers. Still feeling anxious, she went to the chapel and dressed in white. Elder Kristofferson was there, but the reassurance he gave was not enough. If she went with him into the waters of baptism without an answer from the Lord, Anna felt sure she would be going to her death.

Elder Kristofferson stepped down into the water, pleased to find the water not so chilly. The iciness had departed since his prayer and he felt sure this sign meant the Lord would protect his convert. Anna stood above him, her face pale and frightened. He reached up a hand to help her down into the water, but she merely stared past his head, ignoring the hand. He asked for her full name, but again there was no response. She didn't even glance in his direction. He called to her, but again she stared past him without taking a step forward.

It wasn't until Elder Kristofferson had called her a third time that she stirred, the fear on her face replaced by a bright inner glow. Grasping his hand firmly, Anna stepped briskly down into the water. All went well during the baptism and she was confirmed at the edge of the baptismal font.

Afterwards she explained what had happened as she stood motionless on the steps. Her desire for a firm knowledge of the truth of the gospel had been answered beyond her dreams. In those few seconds when Anna had stood immobile above the water while Elder Kristofferson called to her in vain, she had seen a figure clothed in white, standing at the furthest edge of the font. She had stared past the missionary at this familiar figure who held his arms outstretched toward her. Signaling as plainly as if he had spoken, she felt him say, "Come unto me."

# 5

# Driven Out of Her Home

## Sister Horsley

In the spring of 1849, Sister Horsley's life changed forever when the missionaries came to Cambridgeshire, England, to spread the news of the restored gospel of Jesus Christ. Although her husband didn't want anything to do with the Mormon elders, their message sank deeply into her heart. Within a short time, she had developed a strong testimony.

Unfortunately, as her love for the gospel grew, so did the antagonism her husband and parents felt toward the Church. Her husband became so alarmed when she announced that she wanted to be baptized that he brought over the minister of his church to try to talk sense into his errant wife and to persuade her not to join.

"Join anything, but keep away from the Mormons," her husband often told her bitterly. Although he continually derided her doctrine, she remained true and steadfast and after a time insisted on being baptized.

After her baptism, their relationship deteriorated all the more, and the once-happy couple began arguing frequently. William, their young son, cried when he saw his father verbally and sometimes physically abusing his mother. Daily, his father's mood became more terrible.

H

One morning Mr. Horsley told his wife that the time had come for her to make a final decision. She had one last chance, he said. Either renounce Mormonism and stay a part of his household, or continue to embrace Mormonism and leave. Trembling, she replied that she could not give up her faith. Striding to the door, Mr. Horsley flung it open. Although his wife stood clutching an infant in her arms and their sobbing six-year-old son stood beside her, he pushed his wife outside and slammed the door. William clung to his mother's skirts as she stumbled down the street crying.

She walked to her parent's home and became despondent when they refused to let her enter because she was a Mormon. Finally, she found a friendly Latter-day Saint couple who let her in. That night, William cried and begged her to return to the home where he had once been so happy and comfortable. "No my boy," she patted his head, declaring sadly, "never will I give up what I believe to be the truth; no, not for all the homes of this world."

The next day, she traveled to London where her three sisters lived. Each had comfortable homes, and she felt assured of a welcome. But she was thunderstruck when each sister, one after the other, turned her away. Her bitter parents had already contacted them, and now they would have nothing to do with her. She felt as if her heart would break. Homeless and with no money for food or shelter, Sister Horsley began to panic, wondering how she could take care of her small baby and young son. She went back to one sister's home and begged her to keep William until she could find a place to stay.

For days, she wandered about London, hungry and homeless until she was able to get a job sewing at a tailoring shop. The hours were long and tedious and the pay minimal, but at least she could support herself. After a few weeks, she returned for her son. When she took William to her tiny apartment, he was shocked at the bare, ugly room, being used to a luxurious home, but he soon settled in.

Despite his youth, William decided after some weeks to help earn money. He got a job as a stationer. It was his duty to watch the news stand from 8 A.M. to 8 P.M., for which he was paid two shillings and six pence, which was about sixty cents a week. When William brought home his first week's pay, his mother hugged him, tears running down her face.

"God bless you my boy," she cried, kissing him.

Trouble came a few weeks later in the form of her husband, who soon discovered where his family was staying. He tried again and again to make his wife renounce the gospel. When he failed, he began to harass her.

William stated, "His persecutions became almost unbearable, until one day he tried to take me to my old home by force." With the boy kicking and yelling and the mother fighting desperately, he gave up and ran away. However, the next day, at work, William spied his father across the street furtively watching him. The boy quit his job and got another in a different locale. He had to change jobs twice more after that as, each time, his father discovered where he worked.

Sister Horsley became frantic about the situation, fearing that her husband planned to snatch the boy. Her future plans included migrating to Utah, but she didn't have enough money saved for them all to go at present. Under these desperate conditions, she decided to send William on ahead to Utah with a gentleman who promised to look after him, telling her little son that she would follow as soon as she could earn the passage for herself and the baby. Eyes brimming with tears, Sister Horsley tried not to despair on April 6, 1855, as her young child boarded a ship that would carry him across the ocean. She had reason to fear.

Soon after crossing the plains, William's guardian decided to go back East. He left him with George Openshaw, a penniless man who cared little about the young boy. William lost contact with his mother and having no permanent home, wandered from place to place.

The boy's distraught mother never gave up searching for him, but she was hampered by distance and began to wonder if she would ever find him. In the spring of 1857, Sister Horsley talked with a man who was going to Salt Lake City and begged him to try to find her son. Miraculously, the man was able to locate William and took him in, but he was verbally and physically abusive to the boy. A neighbor became aware of poor William's plight and kindly took him into his own home.

It wasn't until the fall of 1860 that Sister Horsley was able to travel West and be reunited with her son. They moved to a home in Salt Lake City where she continued to make her living by sewing and tailoring. At last, she had her family together and was happy and free to practice her religion. Despite the persecution and hardship she had endured in England, her testimony of the gospel remained strong and unwavering.

# 6

## Baptism in a Therapy Tank

Joel Norris

Joel Norris was lying in a hospital in Gainesville, Florida, being examined for possible tumors, when his wife met with two elders from The Church of Jesus Christ of Latter-day Saints. She asked Elder Shane Rowley and his companion to visit her husband to try to help raise his flagging spirits.

She cautioned them that he would not be interested in the Church, as he belonged to another. But she thought it might be helpful if they went and talked with him at the Veteran's Hospital. Elder Rowley said, "We visited Joel that day and just talked with him and listened to his life story." An easy rapport developed between the three men. As they were ready to leave, Joel invited the missionaries to return for another chat.

The elders began visiting him every other day, working it into their busy schedule. An interesting coincidence developed. "It seemed that every time we went to visit him, a member of his church would be there to try to start an argument." However, the missionaries were careful never to argue or say anything contentious. Later, Joel confided that their remarkable attempts to avoid any type of confrontation softened his heart toward the gospel. He was impressed that they refused to quarrel or even debate and felt that the elders spoke with power and truth.

The missionaries hadn't been meeting with Joel for very long when the doctors delivered a grave diagnosis. He had malignant tumors. Not only were they in his head and spinal column, they were also in one lung and in a leg. Life expectancy was less than a year. Elder Rowley and his companion were shocked at the news and disturbed by Joel's fearful reaction. He was terrified of the idea of dying.

The doctors said they would operate and remove the tumors in his head and spinal column. The delicate surgery would require taking a piece of bone from his lower leg and inserting it into his back to support the vertebrae when the tumor was cut out. However, Joel's fears increased when the doctors didn't appear hopeful about the outcome.

On the eve of the operation, Joel asked the missionaries to administer to him. Elder Rowley stated, "We gave him a blessing and promised him he would completely recover." After the blessing, Joel was still fearful but said he felt a new spirit of peace.

The operation was long and difficult, but Joel survived, though he was on the edge of death. After weeks in intensive care, he was placed on a special Stryker frame and was not allowed to move at all, not even an inch. The doctors feared that if he moved his spine would collapse.

The elders continued to go to the hospital, teaching him the discussions. With each meeting, they felt the Holy Spirit attending. Finally, Joel began testifying to friends in his own church that he knew The Church of Jesus Christ of Latter-day Saints was true and that the power of the priesthood was real.

The time came for the elders to challenge him to come into the Church. Tears fell from Joel's eyes as he accepted, thanking the young men for bringing him the gospel. There was only one problem: he wanted to be baptized immediately. This posed a great dilemma for Joel's family and for the doctors. He had not recovered enough to be taken off the Stryker frame, and the slightest movement could severely injure him. Joel asked if it were possible to be baptized in a therapy tank, where he could remain strapped to the frame.

While theoretically it could be done, the doctors were loath to agree. Yet Joel continued to persist, finally wearing the doctors down until they gave their reluctant permission.

On the day Joel was to be baptized, the elders held their breath as he was slowly and carefully placed in the therapy tank, still attached to the Stryker frame. He was baptized in a moving ceremony. Elder Rowley said, "If he had slipped at all, he might have died, or at least, have been paralyzed for life." Joel was confirmed a member of the Church shortly after.

Joel went on to recover—to the astonishment of his doubtful doctors—and became an active member of the Church.

# 7

# Rescuing the Handcart Company

Ephraim K. Hanks

Ready for a good night's sleep, Ephraim K. Hanks prepared for bed. He had just drifted off when a voice startled him, bringing him fully awake. Groggily, Ephraim looked around to see who had spoken. There, in the doorway of the bedroom, stood a personage of medium build. Astonished, Ephraim rose slightly as the angelic visitor asked a solemn question:

"The handcart people are in trouble and you are wanted. Will you go and help them?"

Earlier that day in 1856, while in Utah Valley, Ephraim had felt impressed to go to Salt Lake City. He felt that for some unknown reason the Lord wanted him there. He had set out on his journey, and it was dark when Ephraim reached Draper, a town thirty miles south of Salt Lake City. He decided to stay overnight with a friend, Gerney Brown, glad for a chance to visit. But he was so tired from traveling that he had said good night early. Then, the angel woke him with his solemn question.

Ephraim answered with equal soberness. "Yes, I will go." The personage left, and, thinking that he had settled the matter, Ephraim turned over and went back to sleep. A few minutes later, the voice roused him once more, asking the same question:

"The handcart people are in trouble and you are wanted. Will you go and help them?" Ephraim answered firmly that he would and again the personage left. He made himself comfortable and went back to sleep, only to be roused a third time when the visitor once more repeated the request for help. Clearly, this angel meant business and Ephraim obediently got up out of bed and dressed. Sister Brown fixed him some food. He began his journey to Salt Lake City in the dark hours of early morning.

After daylight, he was surprised to meet a messenger from President Brigham Young who was on his way to fetch Ephraim Hanks to help the handcart people. The messenger was glad to know that an angel had saved him a long ride. The next day, in Salt Lake City, Brigham Young asked for other volunteers to rescue the desperate pioneers, and the brethren quickly made plans. Some stated they could finish their business, load up with supplies, and be ready to leave in two days.

However, remembering the angel's insistence, Ephraim spoke up, "I am ready now." He spent the rest of the day making his preparations. He set out alone the next day in a light wagon.

About ten miles east of Green River, Ephraim ran into a group of wagons that had left a week earlier to rescue the handcart companies but had been forced to turn back because of deep snow. Because of earlier reports on the dire plight of the people, and because of recent heavy snows and frigid temperatures, the company leaders were all convinced that the immigrants, together with twenty-seven men sent previously to help them, had perished. Gathering additional supplies from their wagons, Ephraim continued on and met up with Reddick N. Allred near South Pass. The men camped there overnight when a tremendous blizzard hit. The snow was so deep it was impossible to move wagons through it.

The long delay worried Ephraim, as he could plainly imagine the hardship this would cause the already suffering Saints. Finally, he could stand it no longer. Borrowing a saddle, horse, and pack animals, he started off in snow that was almost up to his waist. On the way, he met Brother Joseph A. Young and Brother Garr, who had left earlier from Salt Lake City. Despite the terrible snows, they had managed to reach the stricken pioneers. They were now headed back to Salt Lake City with heartbreaking reports for Brigham Young on how the handcart people were literally freezing and starving to death.

Ephraim camped that night in deep snow. When he reached Ice Springs Bench the next day, he was surprised to see a herd of buffalo. It was a rare sight to see those great animals in that particular area so late in the year. Ephraim killed a big cow with one shot. After skinning and dressing it, he cut the meat into long strips before loading it onto two horses.

An hour before sundown, Ephraim looked off in the distance and saw a dark streak against the snow. As he got closer, he could see the line was moving and felt sure it was the Martin Handcart Company. He reached them on the 11th of November, just as they were beginning to make camp for the night.

"About sundown I reached the ill-fated handcart company. The starved forms and haggard countenances of the poor sufferers, as they moved about slowly, shivering with cold, to prepare their scanty evening meal was enough to touch the emotions of the hardest heart. When I saw the terrible condition of the immigrants on first entering their camp, my heart almost melted within me. When they saw me coming, they hailed me with joy inexpressible and when they further beheld the supply

F THOMAS 99

of fresh meat I brought into camp, their gratitude knew no bounds. Flocking around me one would say, 'Please give me some meat for my hungry children!' Shivering urchins with tears streaming down their cheeks would cry out, 'Please mister, give me some!' And so it went. In less than ten minutes the meat was all gone."

Mary Goble was among the suffering pioneers and had watched as her infant sister and mother had died on the trail before help could arrive. Her feet were frozen, and her toes had to be amputated with a saw and a butcher knife. She was overjoyed to see Ephraim ride into camp and tell them Brigham Young was sending help and that they would soon have flour.

She wrote later, "There was rejoicing that night, we sang songs, some danced and some cried. He was a living Santa Claus!"

That evening, as Ephraim sat by the campfire, a weeping woman hurried by with bowed head. Curious, Ephraim followed her to Daniel Tyler's tent, where she begged the man to administer to her sick husband. He agreed and Ephraim joined them, watching as Elder Tyler bent over the woman's husband, then straightened up.

"I cannot administer to a dead man," he said with a pained expression. With those melancholy words came a strong impression to act. Ephraim ran to ask Captain Grant and Heber P. Kimball to help him administer to a sick man. When they arrived at the tent, he had the elders wash the debilitated man with warm water. Then they administered to him and Ephraim commanded the brother in the name of Jesus Christ to breathe and live. Immediately, the man took several audible breaths and soon sat up. His wife was delirious with joy at the miracle. Running out of the tent, she spread the news throughout the camp.

"My husband was dead," she cried, "but the man who brought the meat has healed him!" That was the first of many healings Ephraim would perform that evening. John Jaques, another member of the camp, wrote in his journal about these healings.

"The next morning, everyone in camp was talking about Brother Hanks, about his prayers for the sick, but even more the operations he had performed with his hunting knife. Many of the Saints were carrying frozen limbs which were endangering their lives. Brother Hanks anointed these folks and prayed that the amputation could be done without pain. Then when he took out his great hunting knife, held it in the fire to cleanse it, and took off the dying limb with its keen blade; many with tears in their eyes said they hadn't felt a thing."

These experiences, together with the reassurance that more help was on the way, gave the pioneers the heart to push on toward the Salt Lake Valley. Ephraim stayed with the company, spending his days in a flurry of activity: tending the sick, obtaining water, hunting for food, and pulling the handcarts of those too weak to do so themselves.

People constantly asked Ephraim to administer to the sick and dying, their requests averaging one per hour during his entire time with the immigrants. On occasion, he blessed two hundred people in a single day. Ephraim felt the Lord was with him, lending him strength as he struggled to alleviate the suffering of the stricken. Frequently, when he administered and rebuked the disease, people were healed instantly. In other cases, the afflicted person would immediately begin to rally.

Daily, the company leaders gently urged the pioneers forward, to move as fast as they could. In the morning, as soon as Ephraim had helped the company begin its daily trek, he would leave in search of game. Ephraim and the other experienced scouts marveled at the unusual abundance of buffalo. He was often able to kill one of the huge animals and distribute its meat among a thankful people. Ephraim pondered upon this phenomenon:

> The most remarkable thing about it was that I had traveled that road more than fifty times and never before saw so many buffaloes in that part of the country. There was not a member of the party but what believed that the Lord had sent them to us in answer to prayer.

One day, a weakened woman became separated from the camp when she fell unconscious. Unaware of her plight, the camp moved on. When her absence was discovered, Ephraim went back to search. He found her, pulled her astride his horse, and carried her back into camp, saving her from certain death in a snowy bed.

The company now began meeting with relief companies sent from Salt Lake City. As they arrived, the Saints put their scanty belongings into the wagons and discarded their handcarts.

Ephraim endured bitter cold, meager rations, arduous work, exposure to the elements, and communicable diseases in order to help his fellow Saints. He literally became a temporal savior to the starved and weakened pioneers. Faithful to his promise to a nighttime angelic visitor, Ephraim remained with the Martin Handcart Company until they reached Salt Lake City on November 30th, 1856.

# 8

## *Food for the Saints*

Joseph F. Smith

Thoughts of attack were far from the mind of nine-year-old Joseph F. Smith as he mounted his horse on a particularly bright fall morning in 1847. Joseph and three other boys were setting out to take a herd of cattle and several pair of oxen to graze. With him was Thomas Burdick, who was near his own size though slightly older, Alden Burdick, Thomas's sober older cousin, and Isaac Blocksome, a boy around eight years old.

The group had started out for the grazing grounds, about two miles away from Winter Quarters, when Alden decided to walk so he could collect nuts through the hazel brush. He directed the younger boys to take the cattle on the brush-free "upper road," while he himself took the "lower road." He told the boys to meet him at the spring.

Joseph and Thomas were glad enough for this arrangement, as it would afford them time alone to play without having Alden chasten them for their youthful antics. Joseph took the lead on Alden's bay mare and Thomas followed, riding a black pony. Isaac was left with Joseph's handicapped horse.

The boys found it vastly amusing to tickle the younger boy's pony with sticks, making it jump and lunge. Isaac hung on as the boys made the animal buck and run until finally Isaac burst out in frustrated tears. Angry about the teasing, the young boy finally slid off his mount and headed home on foot. Joseph and Thomas shrugged it off.

After reaching the spring, the two boys put their lunch pails in the water to keep cool, then leaped back on their horses. They raced each other over the flat, jumping over holes and scaring themselves as they clutched at the horses' manes to keep from falling. While the boys played, the cattle grazed calmly about half a mile away near the spring at the foot of a hill. Suddenly a band of Indians appeared.

Thomas immediately swung his horse around and turned for home, crying loudly, "Indians!" Meanwhile, Joseph stared at the cattle, which were on the verge of being taken. Many thoughts coursed though his brain, but foremost was the long journey to the Salt Lake Valley in the spring. They would be in great need of the food the cattle could provide. His mother, brother, and sisters were dependent upon those animals, as were the other saints. He had to save the cattle!

Making a quick decision, Joseph dug his heels into the sides of the bay and raced to the cattle, intending to turn them toward home. Unfortunately, the Indians reached the leaders of the herd at the same time. Sawing at the reins, Joseph pulled up and swung his horse round, whooping loudly at the cattle. Spooked by all the commotion, the animals began stampeding in the direction Joseph wanted, toward Winter Quarters.

The Indians split up, some going after Thomas, who was still sounding the alarm. Joseph glanced up to see his friend jump off his horse when he reached the top of the hill. A tall man snatched up the reins of Thomas's horse as the boy continued his flight on foot. Joseph continued to race alongside the cattle, managing to keep the cattle headed in the direction of the lower road. Although the Indians tried to catch up and head him and the cattle off, his horse was fleeter and he remained ahead.

However, the Indians who had pursued Thomas left off their chase after capturing the boy's horse and rode to meet Joseph at the head of the spring. They managed to turn the cattle around and now all were racing down the stream. When they reached the hill, a group of Indians sprang out, causing the cattle to swerve again in the direction of Winter Quarters.

As they passed the spring once more, Joseph saw another group of Indians in front of him with their horses so tightly bunched together that Joseph could not go through them. He pulled off to the right, intending to go around them. But they turned in the same direction and cut him off. When Joseph pulled to the left, the line of Indians also swung left. Forcing him to cut his speed with these maneuvers, the Indians were able to overtake him.

Two of them rode up alongside Joseph, one on either side of his horse. Each grabbed hold of one of the boy's arms and legs. "They raised him from the saddle, slackened speed till his horse ran from under him, then dashed him to the ground among their horses' feet while running at great speed."

Fortunately, Joseph was only stunned and managed to get to his feet after a few moments. Looking again toward the top of the hill, he saw several men running with their pitchforks. They had been on their way to the hay fields when they were alerted by Thomas's cries. Noticing their arrival, the Indians rode off. For a few minutes, Joseph debated whether to start rounding up the cattle he had saved. As the cattle were so far away, he decided to go and get help.

Worried sick, Joseph's mother and family were overjoyed to see him walk into camp. Two companies were quickly organized to bring in the cattle. Despite his ordeal, Joseph joined them but they could find no signs of the cattle. As they continued to search high and low, Joseph returned to the spring. He found the saddle blanket from Alden's bay mare but noted that their dinner pails had been taken. The men began to return to Winter Quarters exhausted and disappointed. Joseph cried bitterly about the loss.

However, they had forgotten about Alden. He had reached the grazing grounds just after Joseph had turned toward home after his rude jolt on the ground. Alden was alarmed to find no sign of the boys, while the cattle were straying off unattended. Although he didn't know that Indians were present, he knew something was wrong. Deciding to take no chances, he gathered up the dinner pails and drove the cattle home.

Once he arrived, Alden learned the full story. A messenger was sent to inform the search party of the cattle's return, but he was unable to locate the men. On their arrival home, the exhausted men were happy, though a bit exasperated, to learn that the cattle they had spent so many hours searching for had been milling about safely in the corrals. Joseph watched the cattle with delight, receiving many congratulations and back slaps for his bravery in saving them for the Saints.

# 9

# To the Aid of His Brothers

## Samuel H. Smith

People in Carthage had been distrustful and angry at the Saints for some time. But lately their bitter feelings were breaking out in dangerous ways. Samuel Smith was well aware of the extreme passions of the local people when word reached him at his farm in Plymouth that his brothers, Joseph and Hyrum, had been thrown into prison. Unsure that his brothers were cognizant of the treacherous mob spirit that had recently overtaken the city, he felt a responsibility to warn them and do what he could to protect them.

Samuel had been fiercely loyal and solicitous of his older brother ever since Joseph had received his first vision and told his twelve-year-old brother about seeing Heavenly Father and Jesus. More garrulous than Joseph, Samuel seemed to look at life lightly. Like all the Smith brothers, he simply liked people, and people liked him in return.

Samuel was the third man in the Church to be baptized, was one of the Eight Witnesses of the Book of Mormon, and worked on Joseph's farm to allow the Prophet more time to translate. At the age of twenty-one, Samuel had been one of the six who formed the new Church of Jesus Christ. At the first conference of the Church, in

1830, he was ordained an elder. Three weeks later, he was set apart as a missionary. On his mission, Samuel gave a Book of Mormon to a Mrs. Rhoda Greene, who later showed it to her brother, Brigham Young. Another future leader of the Church, Heber C. Kimball, read that same Book of Mormon. Two years after returning home, Samuel went on a second mission.

Persecution was nothing strange to the Smith family, but on this particular day Samuel felt it imperative to reach Joseph and Hyrum. Hitching up a horse and wagon, he started at once for Carthage. Accompanying him was a fourteen-year-old boy who worked for him. He soon discovered that men had set up roadblocks on all roads leading into town and were turning everyone away.

Samuel used all his powers of persuasion to try to talk the men into letting him pass. The guards were almost persuaded, when another guard stepped up and recognized Samuel as the Prophet's brother. All discussion ended, though they let the boy drive the wagon through. They warned Samuel to go back home immediately or they would shoot. He had no choice but to reluctantly turn around.

Samuel went directly to a neighbor's house where he bought a beautiful thoroughbred horse which was known for its speed and endurance. Once again, he headed toward Carthage, determined to get by the guards and help his brothers. Unfortunately there was only one way to get into the city and that was through the blockade. Making his way carefully through the woods, Samuel got as close to the roadblock as he could without being seen. He then kicked his heels into the horse's side and charged forward. The guards flung themselves aside to escape the galloping horse but

F THOMAS 99

quickly recovered. Mounting up, they followed in hot pursuit, shooting wildly.

Urging his horse to tremendous speeds, Samuel dodged bullets during a long and exhausting ride. His superior mount allowed him to elude the guards. When he reached the outskirts of Carthage, a pleasant-looking man stopped Samuel and warned him not to go on. He said Samuel would be killed by a mob that was rampaging through town if he did not go back. Samuel pressed on.

Reaching the jail, his worst fears were realized when he discovered that mobbers had already attacked the men inside, killing his brothers. He had been able to reach the jail only because the mob was now fleeing from the scene. Running up the stairs, Samuel attended to John Taylor's wounds, then helped Willard Richards prepare the bodies of his fallen brothers. Later, with Brother Richards, Mr. Hamilton, and eight guards, he accompanied the bodies eighteen miles to Nauvoo.

After the viewing of the bodies, his mother ministered to Samuel as he was in such pain that he was unable even to sit up. Turning to her, he said, "Mother, I have had a dreadful distress in my side ever since I was chased by the mob and I think I have received some injury which is going to make me sick."

After the funeral for his brothers on June 29th, 1844, Samuel moved to Nauvoo. There he contracted a fever and became very ill. Some believe Samuel sustained some type of injury during his wild ride, as he vomited blood during his last days. Others believe that the extreme physical exhaustion he endured during his pursuit, his taking care of his brother's bodies after the martyrdom, and his distress over their dreadful fate crippled his health.

Samuel's condition quickly worsened. He died on July 30th, at the age of thirty-six. After his death, the *Times and Seasons* wrote a tribute, a part of which reads:

> If ever there lived a good man upon the earth, Samuel H. Smith was that person, in fact he was too good for this generation, and the infinite wisdom of Jehovah seems to have been exerted in this instance of taking him . . . His labors in the Church, from first to last, carrying glad tidings to the eastern cities and finally his steadfastness as one of the witnesses of the Book of Mormon, his many saintly traits of virtue, patience, godliness, brotherly kindness and charity, shall be given of him hereafter as a man of God.

# 10

## *Defending the Missionaries*

### Melford Wallace

As a religious group, the Mormons were still relatively unknown in 1895. This was reflected in Melford Wallace's reply when two young missionaries asked him if he had ever heard of the Latter-day Saints.

"Yes, I remember hearing something about them many years ago." He paused, then continued thoughtfully, "But I thought they had all died off or been killed."

They gladly informed Melford that standing before him were two pieces of evidence to the contrary. It was an inauspicious beginning for the two missionaries who were tracting in Kentucky when a rainstorm hit. The rain drenched their long-tailed Prince Albert coats and the derby hats that were then fashionable.

Feeling sorry for the soaked men, Mr. Wallace invited them to come in and dry themselves before the fire. They continued to talk long after the steam had evaporated from their wet clothes. Their discussion continued so far into the evening that their host insisted they spend the night. They parted the next morning as friends.

The following spring, two other Mormon missionaries, Elders William King and Thomas Martin, came into the area tracting. Mr. Wallace's brother, James M., invited the elders to stay at his home.

When the missionaries made plans to hold a meeting that Thursday evening in Mary Scott's cottage nearby, a group of men heard about their plans and decided to prevent it from taking place. Wednesday night at midnight, a mob appeared in front of James's home to tell the elders they had twenty-four hours to get out of Metcalf County. Despite their threats, the missionaries decided to go ahead with the meeting.

James became increasingly alarmed about the tense situation and rode over the next morning to talk with his brother about how they could help protect the elders.

Thursday evening, Melford attended the meeting at the Scotts' small home, which was filled to overflowing. Members of the mob were scattered among those attending, and though they didn't disturb the meeting, they kept a keen eye on the elders. Near the close of the meeting, Elder King felt impressed to stand. He confessed that there were men who had said that if the missionaries were not out of the county by that night, they would be injured.

Elder King told the crowd that they had been sent to do the work of the Lord and didn't feel they should run away because of threats from men. He paused and looked around the crowd, which had become quite still. Then he added that they needed lodging for the evening. Though he didn't want to bring trouble on anyone, Elder King wondered if there was anyone who might give them shelter for the night.

Melford leaned over and put his hand on his wife's knee. "Mary Ann, I am going to ask those boys to go home with us." Darting an anxious look at the scowling faces of men she suspected of being members of the mob, she bravely replied, "Mel, you know best."

When Elder Martin dismissed the meeting with a firm "Amen," no one moved. The silence was tense as everyone sat eyeing the missionaries. Abruptly, Mr. Wallace rose and strode over to the elders, who sat silently waiting. After introducing himself, he asked if they would like to go home with him. Breathing sighs of relief, the missionaries politely thanked him and rose while the mobbers gave them one final look before slipping quietly out the door. Walking home quickly, the Wallaces frequently darted glances over their shoulders.

It was late when they reached home. Mr. Wallace said to his wife, "Show these boys to their bed at once." When they were out of the room, Melford soberly turned to his sons and to one of their friends who had joined them:

"Because we've invited the missionaries here, we can expect a mob to arrive at any time." Excited, the boys jumped up, eager and anxious to defend the house against attackers. As they started to rush off to fetch their guns, Melford hastily stopped them.

"Hold on boys, that's not quite what I had in mind. I want you all to go immediately to bed and put all your lights out." Their faces dropped, and though they were severely disappointed, they obeyed. A father of many years, Melford decided to ensure their continued obedience by taking all their guns, together with two of his own shotguns and a rifle, to the barn, where he hid them.

When he came back to the house, several of the boys were still up. Having discovered that the weapons had been taken, they began arguing, but their father insisted they go back to bed. He explained that he didn't want guns around because if one of them got excited, it would be too easy to fire. Then the shooting could begin in earnest, and maybe one of the women might get hurt.

Melford made sure everyone went to bed and stayed there. He then put out the lights and went outside to wait for the mob to arrive. After a time, he went closer to the road and, leaning against the fence, smelled the fragrant honeysuckle vine that twined in great heaping masses around the wire.

About 11:30 P.M., the expected masked mob rode up to the gate. The leader began dismounting, then jumped violently as Melford's disembodied voice called out in the darkness.

"Underwood, what do you want?"

Shocked at somehow being recognized, Underwood paused a moment before replying. "You have got those Mormons in there and we have come after them."

Melford kept his voice firm but patient. "Men, I have lived here in this neighborhood for several years. I have always tried to behave myself and tend to my own business. I have never interfered in any of your affairs. Anyone you have seen fit to take into your home was strictly your own affair and none of my business; likewise any person who has come to my home and asked to stay all night, as long as they behaved themselves and acted the part of gentlemen, I have taken care of and that was none of your business." He took a deep breath, and the only sound in the blackness was the chomping of bits and the impatient movement of the horses' hooves.

"Yes, those boys are in my house and asleep and as I see it, they are going to stay there as long as they want to and as long as they behave themselves. My advice to you is to go on home and mind your own business. There are about fifty of you and I think I can call every one of you by name. I know you that well. Now if you think you still want to go in and get them, then it is up to you."

Mr. Wallace stepped back in the darkness and opened the gate, taking care to stay close by the thickly piled honeysuckle vine. The leader turned to one of the other men.

"John Mell," he stated in a flat voice, "I am going home; I don't believe Mr. Wallace would like it if we went in there." Pulling on the reins, he turned his horse and rode away into the night, followed by the others who were soon swallowed up by the blackness.

With a sigh of relief, Melford moved his hand away from the glint of shiny metal hidden in the vine and went back to the house. He stayed up the rest of the night to make sure no one slipped back to harm the elders.

It was months later that he admitted to his wife that he was actually more prepared than he had told the mob. Realizing that it would be foolish to try to defend the place with guns on such a dark night, he decided that, should it prove necessary to actively defend the missionaries, he would use a different type of weapon. So, after hiding the guns in the barn, he had picked up his sharp hand axe and concealed it within the tangle of the honeysuckle vine near the gate, within easy reach.

"If that mob had decided to try to come through the gate," he confessed to his wife, "I was going to grab the hatchet and make it kind of expensive for them. I knew I could get ten or a dozen of them before they knew what was happening to them." From that time on, until 1900, when the Wallace family moved to Utah, the missionaries were frequent guests in the household.

An interesting conclusion to this story occurred about a year after the incident. Mr. Wallace's brother, James, was serving a short-term mission for the Church when a man by the name of Lester Porter attended one of his meetings. Afterwards, Mr. Porter approached James and in an extremely determined manner, which left room for no opposition, insisted that James spend the night at his home. The next morning, Mr. Porter explained why he was so adamant about his invitation.

"Maybe you have wondered why I asked you to come and stay with me," he said, looking a bit sheepish. "I will tell you. You remember the mob that went to your brother Mel's place years ago after those two Mormon Elders? Well, I was in the mob and as I was going home alone, I became so weak I fell off my horse. I had three of these spells and fell off the horse each time. Every time I saw what a horrible thing I had taken part in. I did not get home until after 4 o'clock that morning. I made up my mind that if I ever had a chance to help one of those Elders I would do it. You was my chance and now I feel better. I slept better last night, knowing you was in my house, than I have slept for many, many years."

# 11

## Across the Frozen Waters

Andrew Smith

With faces red from the frosty wind, grown men sat down and cried in eighteen inches of snow when, with their enfeebled wives and children, they beheld the obstacle they had to cross—a frigid stream filled with shards of ice and frozen slush. Starved until their weak bodies could barely pull their handcarts, the pioneers felt it was almost an impossible task to ford a mountain torrent waist deep in places and more than a hundred feet wide. It was here that Andrew Smith carved out a memory for himself in the eyes of those debilitated people.

Born in Scotland, Andrew had joined The Church of Jesus Christ of Latter-day Saints in 1851. Five years later, he had emigrated to America with several hundred other Church members. In June of 1856, his group arrived in Iowa, where they spent three weeks preparing for the handcart journey that would take them thirteen-hundred miles across the plains.

In August, they reached Nebraska and spent time mending their carts, getting ready for the remainder of one of the most remarkable trips ever recorded. Brother James G. Willie was captain of the company. Having discovered Andrew Smith to be a most reliable and conscientious young man, he assigned him to aid the women who had no male relatives. Andrew was delegated to do the heavy work for twenty women and their children, helping them chop wood, mend their carts, and perform other tasks too strenuous for them.

On September 3rd, during a heavy rainstorm, Andrew was one of two men asked to remain behind the handcart company to look for a herd of missing animals. Though the men searched a full week, they couldn't locate the cattle. They came near to losing their lives several times before they were able to rejoin the company.

Because of Andrew's warm, trustworthy nature, he became very popular. The captain made him commissary, no easy task in a company low on food supplies. When the handcart company reached the North Platte bridge, some 950 miles west of Iowa City, their provisions were so exhausted that Captain Willie put everyone on half rations. Some of the weaker pioneers had already died for want of nourishing food. The company reached Independence Rock on October 17th and the Sweetwater on the 19th.

It was here that Andrew doled out the last ounce of flour in camp to the hungry people. They had already been devouring roasted rawhide and wild rose berries to sustain their lives, praying all the while that help from the Salt Lake Valley would soon arrive. The next morning, they pulled their rickety carts to the first of the three crossings of the Sweetwater. With scarves wrapped round their heads to protect them from the weather, the pioneers threw up their hands in horror at the sight of the rushing river. Children cried weakly, clinging to their mothers, whose torn coats flapped in the chill wind.

In their fragile condition, it did not seem possible to survive a drenching in the deep, icy waters. It was especially unbearable to think the water must be crossed in three places, though the first was undoubtedly the

worst. The wind was blowing across a foot and a half of snow, picking up several degrees of iciness.

Without being asked, Andrew Smith stepped forward. Picking up a weakened woman, he put her upon his back, instructing her to cling firmly. He plowed into the waist-high icy waters, using a thick stick to steady himself. Setting down his burden, he came back for another. Again and again, he made his way through the river. He helped men pull handcarts through the water when they were unable to do so themselves, tugging with them as wheels became mired in the muddy bottom. He lifted women, children, and even frail men upon his back and made his way across the water of the river till the cold evening hours.

Solomon F. Kimball later wrote of his heroic efforts:

> It was here that the pilgrim Saint of Ayershire, Scotland, hauled cart load after cart load of suffering humanity across that snow-bound stream of the Sweetwater Valley, until the pangs of hunger penetrated every part of his manly being. It was here that the hero of Linister carried on his back delicate men and dying women through that waist deep water of Devil's Gate Gulch, until every fibre in his quivering body was tested to the very limit.

Finally, Millen Atwood, assistant captain of the Willie Company could stand it no more. "Hold on there, Andrew boy," he cried out. "Hold on there. You've done enough, my boy, the Lord knows you've done enough!"

But his heroic task was not yet done. The pioneers had to keep going or die where they were. Andrew went ahead of the group to break trail through the deep snow, making it easier for the others to follow. He was one of the few left who were strong enough to bury the dead. Many of his evenings were spent digging holes or attending to the sick.

Relief came to the company on October 21st, when a group met them, bringing some supplies. But the pioneers

F THOMAS 99

remained in dire straits until they reached Salt Lake City about three weeks later. Five hundred pioneers had left Iowa, and eighty-two were buried along the way. Had it not been for Andrew, the fatalities would surely have been higher.

Solomon F. Kimball further praised the young man: "Andrew Smith, the handcart veteran of 1856, is a man of character, determination, vigorous, God fearing and as tender hearted as a child. He is ready at all times to aid and counsel friends who need his assistance. Thousands of the older members of the Church remember him for this trait with love and respect. . . . Always he has been on hand to defend the cause of Zion, even at the risk of his life . . . and a braver man it would be difficult to find. Probably no person in the Church has passed through more dangerous places than he, and his energy and great faith in the Lord have always brought him through unscathed."

An anonymous author wrote this poem about Andrew:

Through drifting snow this boy would go
With freezing pilgrims on his back.
Through rivers deep, through slush and sleet,
And o'er the hills he 'broke' the track.
He climbed the heights, then sat up nights,
Nursing the sick and burying dead;
His heart would bleed when he would feed
Poor, helpless children without bread.
With dauntless will he fought on still,
Savings the lives of all he could;
Though he could feel his strength of steel
Waning for want of needed food.

With courage and disregard for his own well-being, Andrew Smith helped prevent others from further suffering. He will long be remembered for his willingness to help others at the peril of his own life. He remained faithful throughout his life. In his later years, he served as a guard at the Salt Lake Temple.

# 12

## Inspired Healer

Amanda Smith

Jacob Haun's mill was one of several scattered along Shoal Creek, Missouri. The area was home to fifteen to twenty Latter-day Saint families. While many utilized the mill for grinding their grain, others used it as a stopping place as they migrated to Caldwell County from Kirtland. When tensions over the Mormons increased in October, 1838, the county militia was called out. After the Battle of Crooked River on the 25th, more Saints moved to Haun's Mill for protection.

Joseph Young, the brother of Brigham, arrived on Sunday, October 26th, and met with the people to determine what action they should take. An extermination order signed by Governor Boggs on October 27th added more anxiety to an already tense situation. David Evans, together with several other brethren, decided to meet with the Missourians on the 28th. At that time, a peace treaty was agreed to by both parties, with Captain Nehemiah Comstock promising to preserve the peace. The Mormons let down their guard but quickly reestablished their pickets after learning that another militia was operating only fourteen miles east.

Mr. and Mrs. Warren Smith and their five children were among those using Haun's Mill as a temporary rest stop, arriving the morning of the 30th. Sister Amanda Smith was born in Becket, Massachusetts, one of ten children. She had married her husband when she was eighteen.

The Smiths were living comfortably and happily as the parents of two little girls when Latter-day Saint missionaries came to their area. After listening to Sidney Rigdon, Orson Hyde, and Simeon D. Carter, Amanda was baptized. Her husband was baptized shortly after. They sold their property and went to live in Kirtland, buying a place west of the temple. But with all the trouble in the area, they lost everything, retaining only enough means to outfit their teams to take them to Missouri.

On their arrival, they were met by a mob in Caldwell County. "We were stopped by a mob of armed men who told us if we went another step, they would kill us all." It was only then that they learned about the infamous extermination order. They were told that within ten days every Mormon left in the state would be shot down. The mob looted their wagons and placed a guard around them for three days before finally letting them go.

On they went, arriving at Haun's Mill, where they pitched their tent next to the blacksmith's shop. That afternoon, David Evans led the company in a short prayer. The children went back to playing in the clear sunshine, and the women returned to cooking and cleaning.

At that very time, unbeknownst to all, a mob of between two and three hundred men was marching across the open prairie to the woods north of the mill. Amanda was sitting in her tent about 4 P.M. when she glanced up to see strangers filtering through the trees. Jumping up, she headed next door, intending to warn the men at the blacksmith's shop, but shots began cutting through the air. The brethren shouted to the women and children to run for the woods while most of them ran into the shop.

Amanda looked around frantically for her boys, but they were nowhere in sight. She grabbed the hands of her girls and began running. Looking around, she could see at once that the mob encircled them on all sides except for the creek's border.

"I ran down the bank and crossed the mill pond on a wood plank, ran up the hill on the other side into the bushes and bullets whistled by me like hailstones and cut down the bushes on all sides of me."

Although a number of bullets entered her clothes, Amanda was not injured. Mary Stedwell, who was running beside her, was not so lucky. She was shot in the hand and fell over a log with a cry. Her dress was draped over the fallen tree trunk, visible to the mob. They continued shooting bullets into her dress as it lay over the log that protected her from further injury. Amanda and her daughters sprinted on until they reached the bottomland. They spent the next two hours hiding in fear of their lives, worrying about the others.

It was sunset when the firing finally ceased. Amanda carefully made her way back, passing the body of an old gentleman lying in the field. She reached the mill just as her oldest son, Willard, emerged from the blacksmith shop carrying the limp body of his six-year-old brother.

"Oh, my Alma is dead!" she cried out in anguish, reaching for him. Her older son quickly answered, "No mother, I think Alma is not dead, but father and brother Sardius are killed!"

"What an answer was this to appall me!" Amanda wrote later. "My husband and son murdered, another little son seemingly mortally wounded and perhaps before the dreadful night should pass the murderers would return and complete their work."

No tears would come. Amanda could not cry, in shock from the calamity of losing not only her husband

and ten-year-old son but filled with anxiety for her little boy. Willard carried her youngest son to their tent where he gently laid him upon a bed so they could examine the dreadful wound. It was a ghastly sight for a mother to see. The entire hip joint had been shot away, together with pieces of flesh and bone that had disintegrated before the muzzle of the gun that had been placed to the child's hip.

The night was now dark as Amanda looked up and around her in anguish, not knowing what to do. She could hear the dogs howling over the dead bodies. The bellows of terrified cattle rent the air. The scent of blood covered the area. Outside, Amanda could hear women sobbing and moaning over the loss of their husbands. Children were crying loudly with fear and grief at losing their fathers and brothers.

Fifteen men had been killed outright, and two others were dying. Several more were wounded, while the rest had fled to save their lives. Amanda turned to God in her greatest hour of trial. Her stricken young child lay before her, in urgent need of a doctor when there was none to be had.

"O, Thou who hearest the prayers of the widow and fatherless," she cried. "What shall I do? Thou knowest my inexperience. Thou seest my poor wounded boy. What shall I do? Heavenly Father, direct me!"

Her faithful mother's prayer was answered immediately by a voice that told her to go to the fire which was still smoldering from the bark of the hickory tree that had been burning earlier. The voice directed her to take the warm ashes and make a lye, which she was to pour into a cloth and put into the little boy's wound. As she did this, Alma stirred a little but did not awaken from his unconscious state. Again and again, Amanda saturated the cloth

with the lye and pressed it into the hole where the hip joint had been. Each time, the cloth came away filled with bits of flesh and splinters of bone. Soon the gruesome task was done, and the wound was clean and white.

"Having finished this, [I] prayed again to the Lord to be instructed further and was answered as distinctly as though a physician had been standing by speaking to me."

She was told to make a slippery-elm poultice and sent Willard out to where such a tree stood nearby. Digging a hole to reach the roots, the boy chopped until he had a good supply, then brought them to his mother who made a compress. The wound was so large that it took a fourth of a yard of linen to cover. Once her ministrations were done, Amanda's eyes welled with tears. She cried the tears that had been held back for hours.

All that dark and lonely night, Amanda and her children remained with their dead and wounded. They had no one but God to turn to for help. They didn't know from one moment to the next whether the mob intended to come back and finish their deadly work.

Amanda could not hear the groans of others without trying in some way to aid them. So, into the darkness she bravely went, accompanied by her son Willard. They entered the pitch darkness of the blacksmith's shop, crawling over the heap of dead bodies to locate the wounded whom they could hear moaning. After doing what they could to ease their suffering, they heard faint sounds from outside and went out into the night. By listening carefully, they were able to follow the moans of a man hidden away in the bushes. He had been unable to move because of his extensive wounds, and they helped him as much as they could.

The next morning, Brother Joseph Young came to the scene of the massacre.

"What shall be done with the dead?" he cried out in despair. There was not time to bury them, not with the mob coming, and there were no men left to dig graves. A deep dry well was located nearby, so into this the bodies were laid in haste. There was no time for a funeral service, as the survivors expected to be fired upon at any moment.

When all the men had been attended to and Brother Joseph was carrying Amanda's boy Sardius to the well, he stopped short, his heart swollen with pain. Joseph had accompanied the Smiths to Haun's Mill and knew the boy well, having spent much time playing and bantering with him. The thought of throwing his little friend into the well was more than he could bear. Laying him down, Brother Young cried that he could not throw the boy into that horrible grave. When Amanda looked out to see her son's body lying upon the ground, she left Alma momentarily.

Rushing out she cried, "Oh, they have left my Sardius unburied in the sun!" Returning to her tent, she got a sheet to cover her son. There he lay until the next day when Amanda, with the help of Willard, picked up the board on which he lay and threw him into the well. She then threw straw and earth into the rude vault to cover the dead.

As she continued to tend to her six-year-old, Willard told her some of the details of that fateful afternoon. When the mob had opened fire, Sardius, Alma, and one other boy had crawled under the bellows in the blacksmith's shop, where most of the men took refuge. A few men in the rear of the shop were able to flee outside and get to the woods, but those caught inside were trapped. Rifles poked through the crevices of the log walls and fired upon the cornered men.

Sardius survived the initial attack but was discovered afterwards by two members of the mob. One of them put a rifle near his head and fired. The third boy, under the bellows, received serious wounds and died after three weeks of incessant pain. Willard also had to tell his mother that one of the mob had pulled his fatally injured father across the shop floor in order to yank off his new boots and that he had died moments later.

Though most of the Saints fled the mill area, fearing the return of the mob, Amanda would not think of leaving. She felt she could not move her seriously injured little boy, no matter what threats were made against her. She moved Alma two miles away to the house of David Evans. She resolved to stay there until her boy was well enough to travel. Again she dressed his hip, following the Spirit's directions, and was reminded that in her husband's trunk there was a bottle of balsam. She poured this into the wound and after it had deadened the pain, spoke to her son.

"Alma, my child," she whispered. "You believe that the Lord made your hip?"

"Yes, Mother."

"Well, the Lord can make something there in the place of your hip. Don't you believe he can, Alma?"

"Do you think that the Lord can, Mother?" the boy inquired in simplicity and wonder.

"Yes, my son," Amanda stoutly replied. "He has shown it all to me in a vision."

She then laid him in a comfortable position on his stomach. "Now, you lay like that, and don't move, and the Lord will make you another hip."

The next day, the mob came and told Amanda and the few other widows who were staying with her that they had to leave the state, or they would kill them and the children. The women tried to explain that there was no way to go, as the mob had taken their horses, wagons, provisions, and spare clothing. Yet, even if she had a wagon, Amanda had already decided she would not risk moving her critically wounded boy. He continued lying down as directed by his mother and she attended to his nursing constantly, never leaving him day or night.

From time to time, messages were sent from the mob warning them to leave or face the consequences. Prayer meetings were held, at which Amanda and the sisters exercised great faith in the Lord. They witnessed the power of God directly as their sick and wounded were healed in amazing ways. Still, their losses were great, and the women spent much of their time in vocal prayer.

Their prayers were not only audible but annoying to the militia camped nearby. One day, a man came to their door with a message from the captain, stating that if she and the other women didn't stop their praying, the captain would send down a posse and kill every one of them.

"Our prayers were hushed in terror," Amanda related. "We dared not let our voices be heard in the house in supplication. I could pray in my bed or in silence but I could not live thus long. This godless silence was more intolerable than had been that night of the massacre."

Amanda so craved to hear her own voice in petition to Heavenly Father that finally she could bear it no longer. That night, she stole down into a cornfield. Crawling into a "stout" of corn, she prayed aloud, stating that the pile of corn was like a temple to her at that moment. When she emerged, Amanda heard a voice speak to her, a voice as plain as she had ever heard.

"It was no silent, strong impression of the spirit," she states firmly, "but a voice repeating a verse of a hymn."

F THOMAS 99

That soul who on Jesus hath leaned for repose,
I cannot, I will not desert to its foes;
That soul, though all hell should endeavor to shake,
I'll never, no never, no never forsake.

That special experience renewed her courage, and from then on Amanda was fearless, feeling that nothing could hurt her and that the Lord would protect her.

Alma continued to lie motionless on his bed, according to the Spirit's direction. Then word came from the mob that unless she and the children were out of the state by a certain day, they would all be killed. Courageously Amanda stayed put, knowing that her son had to lie still in order for God to give him a new hip. The days passed and time ran out. It was the evening of the appointed day when fifty armed men came to the house to execute the sentence. Sister Smith met them at the door.

When they demanded to know why she was not gone, Amanda asked them to enter and see their work. She took each of the men to her little boy's bed, letting the men file by one by one, until all had seen her "excuse" for not leaving. The men went outside and gathered in a tight knot where they began to quarrel among themselves, coming near to fighting each other. Amanda watched through the window as the main group mounted up. They left behind two men, the two she assumed had been left to kill her and her children. They knocked at the door, and when she bravely opened it, she was astonished to hear them ask if she had any meat in the house. She told them no.

"Could you dress a fat hog if one was laid at your door?" they asked gruffly. She replied affirmatively and a short time later they returned, dropped a hefty dead hog on her doorstep, and left. Once again there was meat for her family.

Amanda continued to nurse Alma in the coming weeks. One day, she was out of the house getting a bucket of water when she heard the children screaming. Dropping the bucket, she ran frantically into the house, expecting some disaster but stopped short in amazement. Alma was out of bed. Not only was he standing, he was dancing around as his brother and sisters screamed in joy and astonishment.

He had fully recovered. A flexible gristle had grown in place of the missing joint and socket. His healing remained a mystery and a marvel ever after to physicians. Alma never suffered the least impairment. As an adult, he traveled extensively as a missionary, a living testament of the power of God and the bravery of his mother.

Amanda's heroism had allowed her to stand by her son at the peril of her life and helped heal him through the power of God. But now she needed to get her family out of the state. Toward that end, she traveled ten miles to see Captain Comstock and demanded that he give her back her horses, one of which she could see in his yard. He told her she could have it for five dollars.

Amanda told him that she had no money, knowing he was already quite aware of that fact. The captain's wife jumped into the conversation and angrily declared that the women and children should have been killed too. Aghast, Amanda turned to leave, but as the door closed, she decided instead to go around to the corral. Quickly she cornered her horse and returned home with it.

But one horse was not enough, and when Amanda learned that another one of her horses was at a nearby mill, she traveled there to insist that it be returned. By a strange coincidence, Comstock was also at the mill, yet did not chide her for taking her horse out of his corral. Better yet, when she asked for the second horse, he gave it to her freely, then asked if she had any flour.

"No," she replied. "We have had none for weeks."

He then gave her fifty pounds of flour, some beef, and even filled a can with honey. Although all the food had been taken from the stricken Saints, she was glad to have it for her family. On February 1st, 1839, they started for Illinois.

Although Amanda and her four children suffered much, she continued on with unshaken confidence in God. Later that year, she married again and over time had three more children. She saw the Nauvoo Temple completed and had her ordinance work done, as did her son Willard. Amanda became one of the first members of the Relief Society when it was organized by Joseph Smith. She later traveled to the Salt Lake Valley, where she continued true and steadfast in the gospel of Jesus Christ.

# 13

## "My Heart Never Knew Fear"

### Jacob Hamblin

Jacob Hamblin was called to be a missionary to the Lamanites in southern Utah in 1854. Because of his devotion to the gospel and high moral principles, he gained a reputation for unshakable honesty and the Indians learned to trust him. Besides teaching the gospel, Jacob worked diligently as a peacemaker. His strict policy of always treating the Indians fairly helped to bring about many peace treaties.

However, late in 1874, one treaty appeared to be broken because of a catastrophe that occurred in Grass Valley. In December, four young Navajo braves were returning home when a blizzard struck. They took shelter in an empty home nearby. But as the storm continued, they became hungry and killed a cow nearby for food. Neighbors heard the shots, investigated, and quickly reported the shooting to the owner of the house. The owner, a Mr. McCarty, was furious and gathered his friends to attack them. Tragically, they killed three and wounded the fourth, who managed to escape.

When Jacob learned of the incident, he knew the Navajos would consider it a gross violation of the peace treaty they had with the Mormons. Even though

McCarty and his friends were not Mormons, they lived in Mormon territory. When word of the calamity reached Brigham Young, he sent a message to Jacob, telling him to go immediately to the Navajos and explain that the Mormons were not responsible.

Jacob asked for volunteers to accompany him, but not a single man would agree to go on such a dangerous mission. In fact, his friends and neighbors pled with him to stay home and make preparations for a reprisal attack. Well-meaning friends also told him Brigham would never have told Jacob to go if the president had fully realized the danger. However, Jacob knew that if he did not go and try to make peace, war would be inevitable. Then, more suffering would be caused for innocent men, women, and children. Besides, the fact remained that the prophet had told Jacob to go, and go he did, all alone.

Jacob had not gone far when his son, Joseph, overtook him and handed him a note. It was from Bishop Levi Stewart, who urged Jacob to turn back. Undeterred, Jacob went on, staying overnight at Pahreah. His son came again with yet another note. It begged Jacob to return, saying he would surely be killed if he went on.

But Jacob stoutly said, "I felt that I had no time to lose. . . . My life was of small moment compared with the lives of the Saints and the interest of the kingdom of God. I was determined to trust in the Lord and go on. It was important to get an interview with the Navajos before the outbreak."

Reaching Mowabby, Jacob found that the miners there had heard of the bitter feelings and had reinforced the area defensively. He needed a fresh horse in a hurry and was offered one by two brothers named Smith, who decided to accompany Jacob.

After sundown, they arrived at the Indian camp. A messenger was sent to inform relatives of the young men about the desired council. Jacob asked to talk to Chief Hastele, who had worked as a mediator in the past. But he was not in the area.

Jacob felt grave forebodings as he was shown to his bed and spent a long and restless night. The next morning was also spent in waiting. Finally, at noon the Indians told Jacob and the Smiths that all the relatives had arrived. Together, they walked to the council lodge which was about twenty feet long and twelve feet wide. A fire occupied the center of the room, the smoke escaping through a hole in the roof. Jacob and the brothers entered first and were directed to the far end of the council lodge.

"Into this lodge were crowded some twenty-four Navajos, four of whom were councilors of the nations." Some of the men were Piutes and they brought an interpreter.

The spokesman opened the council by stating that what Jacob had said about the murder of their relatives was false. He said that Jacob had advised the Navajos it would be good for them to cross the river to trade with the Mormons. Because they believed him, three good young men lay on the land for the wolves to eat while the fourth had come home with a bullet hole. The spokesman detailed the thirteen days the young brave had spent alone, cold, hungry, and wounded, and ended his monologue by telling Jacob he needn't think of going home.

Feeling uneasy, Jacob reached for the three revolvers which he had hung on a thong nearby and passed them discreetly behind his back to the Smiths, cautioning them not to use them unless they absolutely had to.

After speaking for several hours, the Navajos allowed Jacob to speak. He reminded the group of the many years he had been their friend and of his constant striving for peace.

"I told them of my long acquaintance with their people and of my labors to maintain peace. I hoped they would not think of killing me for a wrong with which neither myself nor my people had anything to do, and that strangers had done the deed."

His words had a softening effect upon the older men but the younger braves remained angry. Feeling justice was not being done, several left the lodge, returning shortly with their injured friend. The air became electric as the spokesman, with a flourish, exposed his wounds. Angry faces turned accusingly toward Jacob. One young brave gave a heated argument for avenging their friend, asserting they could do no less than put Jacob to death.

Later, the Mormon peacemaker dryly commented about that tense moment: "For a few minutes I felt that if I was ever permitted to see friends and home again I should appreciate the privilege." He was not the only one nervous. Beside him, Jacob felt one of the Smiths grip his revolver. "Hold still," Jacob whispered, feeling reassurance from the Spirit. "Do not make the first move and there will be no move made."

Then he spoke to the Piute interpreter, but the man was trembling so with fear that he would not translate. After much discussion, the Indians finally stated that they would accept a settlement. They would consider the matter closed if Jacob would sign a note promising that the Mormons would give them one hundred cattle for each man slain and fifty cattle for the wounded man. It was a way to end the matter peacefully. But Jacob knew that if he signed he would be admitting that the Mormons were to blame. He refused.

"Shall I acknowledge by my act that my people are guilty of a crime of which I know they are innocent; and neutralize all the good results of our labors among this people for fifteen years?"

One of the chiefs then pointed at the blazing fire and irately exclaimed that Jacob *would* sign if he were stretched over the bed of coals for a while. Jacob calmly replied that he had never lied to them, nor ever deceived them, and he would not pay for a wrong other people had done.

"Let the Americans pay for their own mischief; I will not sign a writing to pay you one hoof." At that point, a Piute chief asked Jacob if he was afraid.

"What is there to scare me?" Jacob answered coolly. "I am not afraid of my friends."

"Friends?" the man bellowed angrily. "You have not a friend in the Navajo nation. Navajo blood has been spilled on your land. You have caused an entire nation to mourn. Your friend, Ketch-e-ne, that used to give you meat when you were hungry and blankets when you were cold, has gone to mourn for his murdered sons. You have caused the bread he eats to be like coals of fire in his mouth and the water he drinks like hot ashes." Pausing briefly, he asked again, "Are you not afraid?"

"No," Hamblin assured him. "My heart never knew fear." This conversation was translated for the Navajos, who were favorably impressed. Jacob had another chance to speak and concluded by saying that he had come on a mission of peace and that the truth could be learned and all differences settled by Chief Hastele, whom everyone trusted.

As the Indians began discussing the situation among themselves once again, the interpreter leaned over. "They are talking good about you now," he whispered.

"I am glad," Jacob replied wryly. "It is time they talked good. What have they said about me?"

"They say you have a good heart. They think they will wait until they see their greater chiefs and believe that the matter will be settled before Hastele."

The tense council lasted twelve hours. At its end, Jacob agreed to go to Mowabby in twenty-five days to meet with Chief Hastele and learn of his decision. Chief Hastele completed a thorough investigation and at its conclusion announced to the Navajos that the Mormons were innocent of the murders.

"I am satisfied. I have gone far enough," he declared. "I know our friends, the Mormons are our true friends. No other people we ever knew would have taken the trouble they have to show us the truth."

Because of the bravery and courage of Jacob Hamblin, a major crisis was averted. This allowed a peaceful ending to a situation that could easily have led to further suffering.

# 14

## "Shoot Away!"

Andrew Free

Standing guard on a ridge near their home, Emmeline Wells, (who later became a wife of Brigham Young), her sister Louisa, and their cousin Eliza Free kept watch for approaching mobs. Because of threats against the Saints, it had been their job during the past three weeks to watch and warn the townspeople of any approaching horde.

Then, early one evening, the girls saw a mounted troop in the distance carrying a red flag. They noted that the group of mobsters was headed toward the mob's camp, which lay some distance from town. The girls listened as the sound of the pounding drums grew louder. They never dreamed that one of the prisoners the mob held was their grandfather, Andrew Free. He was being held for the crime of believing The Church of Jesus Christ of Latter-day Saints was true and refusing to say it was false.

When the mob arrived at their camp, they held a mock trial. It was a sham because the leaders had already decided the fate of the old man. Although he had no friends or family near him for support, Andrew stood firm throughout the ordeal. The captain in charge demanded that Brother Free either renounce Joseph Smith and his religion or be executed on the spot.

F THOMAS '99

"I have not long to live," Brother Free replied firmly, drawing himself up with dignity. "At the worst you cannot deprive me of many days. I will never betray or deny my faith which I know to be of God. Here is my breast, shoot away. I am ready to die for my religion."

With those words, he defiantly pulled his shirt open. The men glanced at each other in embarrassment, unwilling to follow through with their threats. Clearly, they had thought it would be easy to frighten an old man, who was all alone and helpless, into renouncing his beliefs. Instead, the snowy-haired man with the proud bearing made them feel weak and foolish. Not knowing what else to do, the leaders decided to let Andrew think on the matter during the night.

The next morning the elderly prisoner was again brought before the tribunal and asked to forsake his beliefs. Again, Brother Free declared the truth of the restored gospel to all within earshot.

Finally, the captain cursed and declared, "Any man who can be so true to any religion deserves to live." Brother Free was released and went to his home in safety, where family and friends greeted him joyously.

# 15

# *A Courageous Friend*

John Taylor

It takes a true friend to go with another to prison. But then, Elder John Taylor was always loyal to the Prophet Joseph Smith. He loved him as a brother. So it was that on June 27th, 1844, John Taylor was sitting with his friend in a prison cell in the town of Carthage. With them were Willard Richards and Hyrum Smith.

Elder Taylor, a fiery-natured man, regarded their imprisonment as an outrage on their liberties and rights; his emotions churned angrily about the legal travesty.

Finally he blurted out, "Brother Joseph, if you will permit it, and say the word, I will have you out of prison in five hours, if the jail has to come down to do it." His plan was to go to Nauvoo, gather a large force, and bring them back to break the Prophet out of jail. But Joseph refused to let him carry out his plan.

The room they occupied on the second story was one normally kept for the jailer. The atmosphere was melancholy that warm afternoon, and all the men were heavy hearted. In an effort to lift the spirits of the group, Elder Taylor sang "A Poor Wayfaring Man of Grief." When he had finished, Joseph asked him to sing it again.

"I do not feel like singing," he replied gloomily.

"Oh, never mind," Brother Hyrum broke in. "Commence singing and you will get the spirit of it." Brother Taylor could not refuse and shortly after finishing moved to the window. There, he was startled to see a group of men with painted faces rush around the corner to the entrance of the jail. The eight guards stationed around the jail stopped the men, saying they could not pass until they had given up their guns. The mob refused.

As the arguing grew strident and more boisterous, Elder Taylor leaped to the door to fasten it. However, there was only a small, ineffective lock and latch. When the mob reached the door, it soon became apparent that the guards had not disarmed them. One fired into the lock. Hyrum jumped back from the door, too late.

He was shot twice and fell to the floor, exclaiming, "I am a dead man!"

Shocked, Joseph knelt over his brother, crying, "Oh, my poor dear brother Hyrum." Then springing to his feet, he strode swiftly to the door, carrying a pistol Cyrus Wheelock had given him earlier that day. He began firing at the door. When the Prophet moved away, Elder Taylor took his place. Using a hickory cane, he struck furiously at the guns the mob was poking through the door as they shot blindly into the room. Joseph turned to see him courageously defending the door.

"That's right, Brother Taylor," he said encouragingly, "parry them off as well as you can."

Meanwhile, members of the mob were being crushed against the door as more men came crowding up the stairs and pushed forward. The firing became more rapid. Streams of fire as thick as a man's arm were shooting from the guns in the doorway, and the curses of the mob grew to a roar. More and more guns were pushed into the room. When Elder Taylor could not hold them off any longer, he sprang across the room to an open window which was opposite the prison door. A shot fired from the doorway hit him in the middle of his thigh. He felt himself falling and would have fallen outside through the window except that another shot coming from outside struck him in the chest, pushing him back into the room. There, he collapsed onto the floor.

That second shot would have been fatal had it not hit the watch he kept in his vest pocket. Bleeding from his wounds, Elder Taylor managed to drag himself underneath a bed that was near the window.

During his agonized effort to reach cover, three more bullets struck him. One hit him below the left knee. It was never taken out of his leg. The second tore away a chunk of flesh the size of a man's hand from his left hip, spattering the wall with his blood and bits of flesh. Another went into his left arm, just above the wrist.

As Elder Taylor lay helpless, a man shouted, "He has leaped from the window." After the Prophet had fallen through the window, the firing suddenly stopped. Elder Taylor heard the mob pounding down the stairs to get outside. When Willard Richards started to leave the room, Elder Taylor called after him.

"Stop, Doctor, and take me along!" Elder Richards dragged him into an adjoining cell, then looked around helplessly, wondering how to hide him. Not knowing what else to do, Willard laid an old mattress over the injured man.

"I am sorry I cannot do better for you, but that may hide you and you may yet live to tell the tale," the doctor said. "But I expect they will kill me in a few moments." He left to see what had happened to the Prophet. The mob, which panicked after the murders, never returned.

Afterwards, a local doctor was among the townspeople who gathered at the jail. Upon finding that a ball had entered Elder Taylor's forearm and gone downward, lodging in his hand, the doctor took a penknife and made an incision. Then, using a pair of carpenter compasses, he pried out the half-ounce ball. The painful sawing with the dull penknife and awkward prying with the compasses were sheer surgical butchery. The doctor afterwards said that Elder Taylor had nerves like the devil to stand the operation. The people then asked if Elder Taylor would agree to be carried to the Hamilton Hotel where he could be taken care of.

"I don't know you," Elder Taylor replied bitterly, still reeling from extreme pain and shock. "Who am I among? I am surrounded by assassins and murderers. Witness your deeds. Don't talk to me of kindness and comfort. Look at your murdered victims! Look at me! I want none of your counsel or comfort. There may be safety here. I can be assured of none anywhere else."

However, he later agreed to be moved to the hotel, although Dr. Richards was hard pressed to find enough help to move him. Many of the townspeople had fled, fearing that the Mormons would retaliate by attacking the town. A note was sent to Nauvoo to inform the Saints of the murders. When Dr. Richards left Carthage to accompany the bodies of the martyrs, Elder Taylor asked him to take his purse and watch, as he feared the people would steal them.

It was the next day before all of Elder Taylor's wounds could be dressed. His wife Leonora arrived with other brethren. A doctor came from Quincy to further examine Elder Taylor, who was still in great pain. The doctor discovered that a ball was lodged in his badly-swollen thigh and needed to be removed.

"Will you be tied during the operation Mr. Taylor?" he asked.

"Oh no," Elder Taylor responded, "I shall endure the cutting all right."

The ball was buried deep in the flesh, against the bone, and was flattened to about the size of a quarter. Although the operation itself was sheer agony, afterwards he felt relief from the tremendous pain he had been suffering.

The brethren who had remained in Carthage were anxious to get Elder Taylor to a safer place. But his condition was so critical that it was impossible to move him. Some of the townspeople seemed rather eager for Elder Taylor to stay, as a hostage of sorts. They feared that if he left the Mormons would attack the town. However, it was known that there were many in town who wished Elder Taylor were dead.

In an account published later, a lawyer named Backman stated that after Joseph Smith's murder, he personally prevented a desperado from going up the stairs of the jail and killing the wounded Taylor. Others also felt that Elder Taylor should be killed, but they decided that "it was too cowardly to shoot a wounded man." Hearing of this, Elder Taylor remarked, "Thus by the chivalry of murderers, I was prevented from being a second time mutilated or killed."

When Sister Taylor overheard comments from the owners of the hotel that they looked favorably on the murders of Joseph and Hyrum, the brethren decided that even though Elder Taylor was still in serious condition, it was safer to move him than to remain in Carthage. Four days after the martyrdom, Brother Marks, President of the Nauvoo Stake, Dr. Ellis, and several other men brought a wagon to take Elder Taylor to Nauvoo. He was so weak from the loss of blood that he could barely whisper. The doctors of Carthage protested the move, saying it would surely kill him.

Elder Taylor was unable to ride in a wagon, and so a litter was prepared. But the pain from the jolting, even though it was gentler than the bumpier wagon, was too great for him to bear. The men obtained a sleigh and hitched it to a wagon. His wife sat beside him, bathing his wounds with water as the sleigh slipped over the prairie grass. Elder Taylor was thankful to finally reach Nauvoo.

"Never shall I forget the difference of feeling that I experienced between the place that I had left and the one that I now arrived at. I had left a lot of blood-thirsty murderers and had come to the city of the Saints, the people of the living God."

After Elder Taylor's arrival, he was given back his watch. He saw that the watch crystal had been smashed to powder by the ball that otherwise would have entered his heart.

"I shall never forget the feelings of gratitude that I then experienced towards my Heavenly Father," he said after examining the damaged watch. "I felt that the Lord had preserved me by a special act of mercy, that I had still a work to perform upon the earth."

Elder Taylor did yet have a great mission to perform. His untiring devotion and great leadership helped guide and direct the Church. In October of 1880, Elder Taylor succeeded Brigham Young to become the third president of the Church.

# 16

## Saving the Book of Commandments

### Mary Elizabeth and Caroline Rollins

Mary Elizabeth Rollins and her sister Caroline were living in Independence, Missouri, when the local people became determined to make the Mormons leave the state.

"About this time there began to be terrible threats against the Mormons," Mary said. She added that the Latter-day Saints were much too united to suit the inhabitants of Missouri. And because they didn't believe in slavery, people were afraid of them.

In order to force the Mormons to leave the area, mobs set fire to the Saints' homes, barns, and crops. The Rollins home also became a target for the mob. Mary wrote about one incident.

"One night a great many men got together and stoned our house, part of which was hewed logs, the other part or front was brick. After breaking all of the windows, they started tearing off the roof of the brick part amidst awful oaths and yells that were terrible to hear." About that time, a neighbor, Bishop Partridge, was tarred and feathered in the streets.

A few weeks later, Mary and Caroline watched another mob striding through town, bent on destruction. This one broke into the two-story Church printing office which was located near their home. The girls crouched by the corner of a fenced yard and watched as the mob threw Brother W. W. Phelps and his family out of their home. They were forced to watch helplessly as the mob heaved all their furniture out into the street. They then went upstairs and began throwing out the printing equipment that was used to publish materials for the Church. Members of the mob leaned out the window, tossing out everything they could lay their hands on, including the paper on which was printed the Book of Commandments, later called the Doctrine and Covenants.

"My sister Caroline and I were in a corner of the fence tremblingly watching them and they brought out a pile of large sheets of paper saying, 'Here are the Mormon commandments!'" Both girls were aghast when the man threw the pages onto the dirt road in front of the house. Mary felt sick to see the sacred writing tossed like garbage onto the street and said, "I was determined to have some of them." Quickly, she whispered her plan into the other girl's ear.

"They will kill us!" Caroline protested, but she agreed to help.

They intently watched the mob, waiting for an opportunity. It came as the men moved slightly up the road away from the girls. Catching up their skirts so they could move freely, the sisters ran to where the papers lay scattered on the ground. Frantically, they snatched them up, turned swiftly and scurried around the corner of a building.

But they had been spotted. Just as the girls began racing around the corner, clutching the papers, some of the men turned back. One of them spied the two girls. Shouting to them to stop, the man alerted his friends.

W.W. PHELPS
PRINTING CO.
F. THOMAS 99

Several ran after the fleeing girls, who ran for their lives. Mary and Caroline tried to lose their pursuers by squeezing through a hole in a wooden fence and dashing into a cornfield to hide.

"The corn was five or six feet tall and very thick; they hunted quite a while for us, coming very near and making our hearts beat faster."

When the girls had gone on some distance, they stopped. They put the papers on the ground and laid flat upon them, praying they wouldn't be discovered. As the men in their stout boots crunched their way through the cornfield, the girls wondered if their loudly pounding hearts would give them away. The mob searched the field, coming so close at times that Mary could see the men's feet as they stomped through the cornstalks. However the Lord protected them and the men finally gave up their search.

When all had been quiet for some time, the girls rose and gathered up their papers. But they had lost their sense of direction.

"We tried to find our way out but the corn being so high, we could not see where to go." It took a long time to find their way out of the huge cornfield. They came out near an old log stable and saw that Sister Phelps and her children were going in and out, carrying brush and piling it on one side of the barn to use for beds that night.

Relieved to see her, the girls told her how they had managed to save some of the manuscript. Sister Phelps took the sheets and later had them bound into books, giving each of the brave girls a copy. The books were treasured by Mary and Caroline, for they were a reminder of how they had defied a mob in order to save the papers from destruction. Today, their copies are the only original ones in existence.

# 17

# A Friend in Need

Sol Hale

It was far too risky a venture the men thought as they shuffled their feet, refusing to meet Tom Hale's questioning eyes. When they did raise their eyes from the ground, it was to dart quick looks at each other even as their tongues remained silent. Tom turned his back on them. Followed closely by his nine-year-old son, Sol, he went into the house, disgusted that not one man in the group had answered his plea for a volunteer to help save the life of a young Indian family.

Only hours before, a young chief with his wife and baby had come to the Hale home for help. Tom Hale was widely known for his honesty and fair dealing and had been nicknamed Strong Arm because of his terrific grip in wrestling.

The young Indian had glanced anxiously behind him. "Hide us quickly Strong Arm," he exclaimed. "I am Arrowpine, the Ute Chief. The Shoshones are after us." Tom quickly pulled them inside. Yanking back a rag rug, he revealed a hidden trap door. He helped Arrowpine's wife and baby climb down into the cellar, with Arrowpine following after. It wasn't long until a band of Indians rode their sweat-covered ponies into the yard.

F THOMAS 1999

"Have you seen two Indians come this way?" they asked. Tom paused, briefly thinking of the motto he had always lived by and drilled into his son, "Never lie to an Indian." Hesitating, Tom looked off to a distant hill. When the men followed the direction of his eyes, they saw a cloud of dust and curiously looked back at Tom, who seemed to be staring at it. They exchanged knowing glances and nodded to each other smugly, believing that Tom had shown them without words where the Utes were. Pulling their ponies around, they dashed off. Tom went inside to tell the little family the danger was past, and Arrowpine explained what had happened.

"We are here on a visit to Northern Utes and were out by ourselves picking choke cherries when the Shoshones discovered us. They would like to get me . . . because I have often beaten them in battle. My young wife would meet a horrible fate if we should fall into their hands."

"Could you find your way back to the friendly tribe if one of us should lead you by a secret trail to the Northern Road?" Tom inquired.

"Yes," the man said firmly. "We know the way from there and could elude the Shoshones." Tom then stepped outside, where many of his curious neighbors had gathered, and asked for a volunteer to guide the young chief and his family. When none of the men answered his plea, his young son spoke up.

"I'll go Father, I know every step of the way and can be back in a few hours."

His mother was horrified at the thought, but Tom reassured her. "Mother, let him go; he will be as safe as anyone."

Sol's mother fixed a packet of food for them, and they left quickly. Sol kept up an easy lope as he guided the Utes over the trail. When they reached the point where Arrowpine could find his way, the grateful man gravely thanked the youngster for his help. On his way back, Sol kept a sharp watch and returned home safely.

Seven years later, Arrowpine was again in the area with a group of men when a party of inexperienced travelers opened fire and killed one of the Indians. When the local farmers and ranchers heard about the incident, they worried about retaliation and decided to protect their livestock by bringing them to one location. The Hale ranch was chosen as a gathering point. Tom was supervising the influx of animals when he remembered a small herd he had left in the mountains. The other men told him to forget them, that it was too dangerous to get them now. But Sol told his father he would slip up and bring them down.

When sixteen-year-old Sol reached the mountain pasture, the cows were gone, and he decided it would be wise to take the long way home. He was traveling at dusk when his horse shied at a stray calf, which mooed in alarm at the encounter. The hungry Sol followed the calf to its mother in order to get some milk to ease the pangs of his empty stomach. Nudging the calf along, Sol followed its zig-zag course in the darkness. After finding the cow and drinking his fill, Sol was so worn out he bedded down for the night right where he was.

Sol woke up early in the morning. He rubbed his eyes, not believing what he saw in the dim light. The scattered tents with many forms lying on the ground were not a mirage. This was the Indian camp he had unwittingly stumbled upon. There was no hope of escape; he had avoided their attention so far only because of the many animals. Taking a deep breath, Sol arose. He had taken just a step or two before he was seized and taken to their chief.

"What are you doing here and why did you come into my camp?" the chief demanded to know, his face difficult to see in the dim light. "Are you a spy?"

"I came here to find my father's animals."

"Who is your father and who are you?"

"My father is Tom Hale. I am Sol Hale and no spy." When his eyes finally adjusted to the light, Sol saw with surprise that his interrogator was Arrowpine. Hope leaped in him. But when he told the chief who he was, Arrowpine didn't recognize him because he had changed so much in seven years.

"Are you Strong Arm's son? Don't lie to me."

"I do not lie; neither did my father ever deceive you or your people."

"Can you prove to me that you are Strong Arm's son?"

Sol knew he would never forget leading this man and his family to safety. The words fairly tumbled out of his mouth. "Seven years ago when you were hidden in my father's house to get away from the Shoshones, I led you and your young wife with her baby boy through the cedars and along the secret trail to the Northern Road; and I had to run all the way back to the ranch for the Shoshones might have captured me."

In reply to more specific questions, Sol gave significant details of the journey, how they had stopped at a tiny spring to drink and rest a few minutes and what the chief had said as they parted. Still, Arrowpine doubted, until he remembered that there was one item that would prove the boy's identity without a shadow of a doubt. Stepping closer, Arrowpine pulled open Sol's shirt. There, on a leather-woven watch chain, was the grizzly tooth he had given the boy in gratitude for leading him and his family to safety.

"Unbind him!" Arrowpine commanded the others. He then asked, "Would you know your father's animals if you saw them?"

"I could pick them out anywhere."

"Then follow me."

As Sol pointed out his animals, the men separated them from the others. As they did so, a beautiful Arabian mare reared up. Sol caught his breath. The valuable horse had been imported at great expense by his neighbors and was to be used for breeding. This would vastly improve the quality of the local horses. It would be a great loss for the entire community if he did not claim her. Sol reasoned within himself that he should ask for the expensive horse. After all, the Indians were not likely to know or care about her Arabian ancestry. Yet, he also remembered his father's motto to never lie. The men saw him eyeing the mare and waited for him to speak.

After a long pause, he admitted, "She is not ours."

When the animals were collected, some of the braves did not want to let the boy go, and Arrowpine had to talk with them at great length. Finally, he provided Sol with a trusted escort to see him home. When he arrived, Sol found that his father had been out for hours, searching for him.

Many years passed. Sol and Arrowpine eventually met again, this time in Southern Utah.

"Do you remember me, Arrowpine?" Sol asked the older man.

"Yes, you are the son of Strong Arm."

"Can you recollect the morning I claimed my father's stock?"

"Yes, I sometimes think of it."

"Do you recall the fine mare that belonged to my father's friend, the mare that I wanted to claim but did not?"

"I do," Arrowpine said deliberately. "I was watching you."

"Tell me, what would have happened had I claimed the mare?"

"You should have had her, but you never could have got home again."

"Why not?"

"You saw the difficulty I had in restraining my young men. They knew whose animal the mare was and in spite of all I could have done, they would have waylaid you had you attempted to deceive them."

Sol gave quiet thanks for his father's teaching and that he'd had the courage to lead the chief and his family to safety.

# 18

## He Stood Unafraid

David W. Patten

When Elder David W. Patten told Joseph Smith that he had asked the Lord to let him die the death of a martyr, the Prophet bowed his head in sorrow. Joseph Smith said that when a man of Elder Patten's faith asked the Lord for anything, he generally got it.

Elder Patten was one of the first missionaries to go to the Southern states and was well prepared to meet the great task before him. He was a striking figure, built solidly at 6'1", of a dark complexion matched by intense black eyes. When he went with Elder Warren Parrish to preach in Tennessee, the two met with success, though there were some angry mutterings against the Mormons.

Matters worsened at the end of one meeting. Some ruffians went outside and, after receiving encouragement, decided to mob the elders. Elder Patten heard about their threats and quickly strode outside, his piercing black eyes sweeping over the crowd. Without moving a muscle, he told the mob to shoot if they wished. Abashed, the mob quickly dispersed.

Some time later, a group of elders, among them Elder Patten and Elder Parrish, were staying at the home of Seth Utley when forty armed men surrounded the house. The officers had an arrest warrant for Elders Patten, Parrish, and Woodruff.

Elder Wilford Woodruff was in another county at the time and so escaped arrest. He stated, "We were accused in the warrant of the great crime of testifying that Christ would come in this generation and that we promised the Holy Ghost to those whom we baptized."

Elders Patten and Parrish were taken to jail on June 19th, and the trial date was set for the 22nd. On that day, a hundred hostile men gathered to attend the trial, most of them armed. A sham trial commenced. The elders were not permitted to call any witnesses, or even to speak in their own defense. Some did come forward to testify that they had received the Holy Ghost after being baptized by the Mormons. Despite that testimony, the judge pronounced the missionaries guilty.

At the conclusion of the trial, it was normal procedure to allow the defendants to speak. Elder Warren Parrish was permitted to say a few words. But knowing what a forceful orator David was, the judge directly forbade Elder Patten to speak.

That was the final outrage. Stung sharply by the injustice of the situation and heedless of the consequences, Elder Patten rose to his feet and powerfully rebuked the court for the unjust and unlawful trial. Standing above his hostile audience, his complexion flushed with righteous anger, he held the court captive with a searing speech that lasted a good twenty minutes. He listed the abominations they were guilty of, condemned them for their wickedness, and warned them that the curse of God awaited them if they did not repent for arresting two harmless men who were simply preaching the word of God.

The judge was astonished. "You must be armed with secret weapons or you would not talk in this fearless manner to an armed court," he sputtered.

"I have weapons that you know not of," he replied simply, "and they are given me of God, for He gives me all the power I have."

Tired of the whole unsavory matter, the judge decided to get rid of the bothersome elders as quickly as possible. He found them guilty but offered to let them go free if their friends would pay the cost of the court trial. The missionaries agreed to this, mounted their horses, and rode a mile back to Seth Utley's home.

Soon after the elders had gone, however, the mob suddenly changed its mind. They decided that the Mormons had been let off too lightly. A man who had stayed behind overheard the mob declaring that they would make the missionaries pay, as the court hadn't. Quickly mounting his horse, he galloped off to warn the missionaries. He arrived at the Utley home just slightly ahead of the mob.

Given this brief warning, Elders Patten and Parrish were able to escape into the woods moments before the mob, which followed them into the timber. The missionaries were able to keep ahead of their pursuers and, when darkness fell, they felt they were out of danger. They sought shelter at Brother Albert Petty's home and quickly retired.

During the night, Elder Patten woke with a start. Fresh in his mind was a dream in which he was told the mob was on its way to Brother Petty's home and would be there shortly. Brother Patten knew it was a warning to leave the house quickly, so he woke his companion and they hurriedly made their escape. Minutes later, a mob surrounded the house, frustrated that the missionaries had already left.

Elder Patten continued his missionary efforts, doing all he could to further the work of the restored gospel.

F THOMAS 99

Then, in October of 1838, trouble came to the Saints at Far West. A band of mobbers began destroying their property, in many cases driving them from their homes. On the 24th, a member's home was looted and three brethren were taken prisoner. As the Saints appealed to the law for authority to right this wrong, Judge Higbee ruled that the Mormons could legally form a militia and send out a company to disperse the mob and rescue the men. Seventy-five men volunteered, and Brother Patten served as their leader.

On October 25th, 1838, the Battle of Crooked River took place, during which Elder Patten was mortally wounded. He was carried back to town, where he met with his wife and friends.

Speaking to his wife he said, "Whatever you do else, O do not deny the faith." Then he whispered to his friends, "I feel that I have kept the faith, I have finished my course, henceforth there is laid up for me a crown, which the Lord will give me."

A short time later, he died. He was the first latter-day apostle to die a martyr for the gospel. President Wilford Woodruff, who was with Elder Patten at his death, said, "Thus fell the noble David W. Patten as a martyr for the cause of God and he will receive a martyr's crown. He was valiant in the testimony of Jesus Christ while he lived upon the earth. He was a man of great faith and the power of God was with him. He was brave to a fault, even too brave to be preserved. He apparently had no fear of man about him."

# 19

## The Whitest of Lies

Laura Phelps

Laura Phelps had faced persecutions herself, fleeing before a raging mob, which drove her family from Jackson County. But she was shocked to look out her door in Far West and see Joseph Smith and his brother Hyrum running from a mob. Earlier, the Prophet had been tarred and feathered. She knew the mob had even tried to force him to drink poison, so she feared what might happen if they caught him. The two men ran up to her open door.

"Sister Phelps," the Prophet cried, "hide us quickly!" Swiftly, she took them inside, rushing them to the bed, where she covered them with a dark curtain. It was only a matter of moments before the mob was on her doorstep.

"Where are they?" the rough men growled. "We know they are here, we saw them come." Tongue-tied at first, Laura tried to stay calm.

"No, gentlemen, they are not here, but you are welcome to look all you want to." Then Laura looked past them, as if watching someone off in the distance. Wondering what she was eyeing so furtively, they turned to look over their shoulders. Then, as one body they dashed off, sure that she had been watching Joseph and his brother run away. The Prophet came out from hiding and put his hands gratefully on her shoulders.

"Sister Laura, there are black lies and white lies and that certainly was a white one that came from your lips."

Their reprieve was short lived, however. Soon after the Battle of Crooked River, in October, 1838, Joseph and Hyrum were arrested and thrown into jail. Also imprisoned were Laura's father, her husband Morris, Parley P. Pratt, and others. Chained together, the men were marched to Ray County and put in prison at Richmond.

While there, the rude jailers entertained each other with obscene jokes, blasphemies, and filthy language. Parley P. Pratt said they seemed to enjoy telling outrageous and disgusting stories of atrocities they had committed against the Mormons, including robbery, murder, and brutal rapes.

"I had listened till I became so disgusted, shocked, horrified, and so filled with the spirit of indignant justice that I could scarcely refrain from rising upon my feet and rebuking the guards," Elder Pratt recorded later, "but said nothing to Joseph . . . although I lay next to him and knew he was awake.

"All of a sudden, he arose to his feet, and spoke in a voice of thunder, or as the roar of a lion, uttering, as near as I can recollect, the following words: 'Silence, ye fiends of the infernal pit! In the name of Jesus Christ I rebuke you and command you to be still; I will not live another minute and hear such language. Cease such talk, or you or I will die this instant!'

"He ceased to speak. He stood erect in terrible majesty. Chained, and without a weapon; calm, unruffled and dignified . . . he looked upon the quailing guards, whose weapons were lowered or dropped to the ground; whose knees smote together, and who, shrinking into a corner, or crouching at his feet, begged his pardon, and remained quiet.

"I have seen the ministers of justice, clothed in magisterial robes, and criminals arraigned before them, while life was suspended on a breath, in the Courts of England; I have witnessed a Congress in solemn session to give laws to nations; I have tried to conceive of kings, of royal courts, of thrones and crowns; and of emperors assembled to decide the fate of kingdoms; but dignity and majesty have I seen but once, as it stood in chains, at midnight, in a dungeon."

Laura's husband, who had witnessed this scene with awe, later related the story to his wife.

General Lucas wanted to have the Mormon leaders killed at that time. Their lives were spared, however, though Joseph and Hyrum, as the leaders, were taken to Liberty Jail. The others remained at Richmond. When Sister Phelps tried to find out what the charges were against her husband, all the authorities would say was that he had gone partway to the Battle of Crooked River.

The prisoners' food was terrible, consisting mostly of bones with tiny bits of meat attached and coarse cornbread. There was so little food that the men would have starved had not their wives brought some. In a desperate attempt to win the authorities' compassion and secure her husband's release, Laura took her infant and moved into prison with Morris for days at a time. Later, the men were moved to Boone County, Missouri. In order to cope with the loss of her husband, Laura asked for a patriarchal blessing at the hand of Joseph Smith Senior.

In February of 1839, Joseph and his companions were able to escape, but this proved detrimental to those still imprisoned. The prosecutors swore in their anger that they would keep the men incarcerated in Boone County.

Morris had languished in jail for approximately six months while between twelve to fourteen thousand Saints were expelled from Missouri. Laura drove her own team and settled for a time near Montrose, Iowa. She cleaned out an abandoned house that had been used to stable horses so as to provide shelter for her children. She paid the rent by selling her books.

When Laura received word that her husband was ill, she asked a woman to stay with her children while she journeyed to Nauvoo. She went to inquire of the Prophet whether she would be of help by going to Missouri for her husband's hearing, which was to be held shortly.

"Sister Laura, perhaps you can accomplish more than we can," he allowed. "We have tried our best to get those prisoners liberated, but all our plans have failed." He then gave her a blessing and encouraged her to go.

Thus, Laura Phelps began a journey of over 150 miles into hostile territory, accompanied only by her younger brother John. Recent rains had caused the rivers to swell, and some were dangerous to cross. They reached one river only to find rescuers pulling a drowning man from the waters. They were told not to attempt the crossing. John eyed his sister closely, and when he asked if they should try, her response was quick and affirmative. Tying her horse's halter to his horse's tail, John loosened their girths and told her to say a prayer. Laura knelt on her sidesaddle, tucking her skirts around her.

The horses inched into the water, which was soon knee deep. Suddenly, they began to swim. Frightened by the current that was wild and swift, John's horse began thrashing as it tried to turn back. But John was able to force him forward, though the animal had pulled them far downstream from the spot where he had hoped to land. If they continued their present angled crossing, they would face a drop off, which meant certain disaster. Laura realized their danger and urged her horse against the other's flank, forcing it upward. Finally, they reached the bank safely.

At the jail, Brothers Phelps, Pratt, and Follett looked haggard after eight months of imprisonment. Another man was with them, but as he was a spy planted by the jailer, he received much better treatment. All three men had been sick and were near despair, as their jailers kept boasting about having prisoners' cases postponed for years. The men rejoiced to see Laura and John as well as Parley's brother. Orson Pratt had arrived on July 1st to be present for the hearing also.

When they went to the court building for the hearing, no one appeared against the men, so they were returned to jail feeling despondent. Now, they decided, it was time for action.

With Laura's arrival, the Lord had prepared a way for the three men to be delivered. Both Laura and Parley received visions of a way for them to escape. Although she was frightened of the possible consequences, Laura was determined to help Morris and the others.

"Faith serves as a dynamic force . . . and as an anchor," she said later of her determination to assist her husband. She had agreed to play a risky part in helping them break out of jail.

Parley stated it would be her job "to lull them [the guards] into serenity, and also of furnishing a third horse, as there were three of us."

Near sunset on the appointed evening, Orson and John pretended to start for home, taking Laura's horse and telling the jailer they were going to leave Sister Phelps with her husband. They tied up the horses a short distance away and waited for the sun to go down.

That was the only time of day the prisoners could escape, as after dusk they were locked in the lower dungeon. Laura sat in the kitchen with the jailer and his wife.

"Well, I must give the boys their supper," the jailer said at the appointed time of night. That was the signal. Parley recounted that each had their individual parts to play at that moment: Laura was to pray; Brother Follett was to push the door open wide when the jailer unlocked it; and Morris, who was a skilled wrestler, was to charge out and engage the jailer. All went according to plan until the jailer's wife, all two hundred pounds of her, grabbed two of the men. She began screaming for help, while her husband wrestled with Brother Phelps.

"Lord, God of Israel, thou canst help," Laura cried aloud. Brothers Pratt and Follett broke free, but Morris was still struggling.

Laura thought she was praying silently, but her husband told her later that she had shouted, "Oh Lord God of Abraham, Isaac and Jacob, deliver thy servant!" Just then, Morris slipped free. He followed the others in a mad dash to the woods in full view of the townspeople.

Hearing the commotion, men came running, grabbing their rifles or clubs. Dogs barked, boys shouted, and cattle bellowed as a posse ran into the woods. Others mounted their horses, jumped fences, breaking them down, tumbling over hedges and ditches. The prisoners fled for their lives. Parley said, "Our toes barely touching the ground while we seemed to leap with the fleetness of a deer."

John and Orson helped the weakened men mount their horses, then placed whips and reins in their hands. "Fly quickly," Orson shouted, "they are upon you!"

"Which way shall we go?"

"Where you can, you are already nearly surrounded."

Sprinting away madly, John and Orson managed to make it to a ravine. There, they hid for a time before making their way to Quincey on foot.

The three prisoners split up. After riding a distance, Parley came to an open area. But as there were men all about, he returned to the forest and tied up the horse before hiding nearby. He felt quite ill and faint for some time. When he returned, the horse was gone. Feeble and weakened by his ordeal, it took Parley a long time to make his way to freedom. He was thankful Laura had thoughtfully put food in his pocket for the journey.

Morris was also pursued but was able to outdistance his hunters. He felt safe until a group of men riding horses approached him from the opposite direction. He was immediately suspected as being one of the escaped prisoners, though the darkness hid his identity.

Drawing closer, the men hailed him in their coarse language, swearing freely. Brother Phelps replied in the same manner of speech, perfectly mimicking their language. He answered them curse for curse about the _____ Mormons who had escaped. Never having heard a Mormon speak in such a manner, and sure that because of his bold and fearless manner he could not be a man fleeing for his life, they apologized for their suspicions.

With speech punctuated with curses, the men told him, "Oh, you are one of the real breed, _____ no _____ Mormon could counterfeit that language." They even complimented him saying, "You swear real natural."

As they talked, Morris continued to imitate their rough speech so perfectly that they shared a few laughs before bidding him a fond farewell to continue their search for the _____ Mormons.

Meanwhile, Laura was left to face the repercussions of their jail break. Parley P. Pratt wrote about her experiences.

"Mrs. Phelps, who was still an inmate of the dwelling, became the particular object of their spite and rage. The old jailer and his wife commenced to rail and curse her as the author of all the mischief. They threatened her with instant death, and finally turned her out of doors in the dusk of the evening, and in the midst of a mob who had gathered in great numbers around the prison, raging like so many disappointed tigers. Being a stranger and without money, friends or acquaintances in the place, she knew not where to go or what to do. She finally sat down in the open air in the midst of the mob, by whom she was assailed, cursed, insulted, threatened and abused in the most unfeeling manner for some time."

However, Laura's thoughts were more upon her husband than her current hazardous position. She wondered fearfully whether Morris had made his way free or if he would be brought back and shot. To her horror, she heard a shout of triumph go up that her husband had been caught. Dancing around Laura, the mob boasted that they meant to roast Morris alive over a slow fire. But when the group of men on horses approached, she saw that it was not her beloved husband but Brother Follett riding her horse. They threw the unfortunate man into prison once more and he spent several more months there before being released.

Exhausted, Laura sank back down as the mob continued to roar and scream against her. Two men came to her rescue, offering to pay for a room at a hotel. But she worried about what people might think of that offer and so refused. A young man saw her sitting there defenseless among all the taunting men. He said outright that he was not used to seeing a woman treated so badly in America. When he went home and told his family, their hearts were touched by her predicament and they hurried to Laura's side.

"Elizabeth," Mr. Richardson said to his wife, "you take this lady to our home. If her husband was the greatest murderer in the world we could not see anyone in our town treated with such cruelty as this."

The Richardsons treated her kindly, going with Laura to the prison the next day and picking up Morris's belongings. After three days, Laura's horse was returned. The Richardsons also cared for the overworked animal. Laura stayed ten days, telling them about the restored Church of Jesus Christ and singing hymns for them. She also gave them a Book of Mormon before saying she had to go. They were horrified, saying it was not safe to travel alone on account of outlaws. But when she insisted, Mr. Richardson made arrangements with the mail boy to accompany her part of the way.

They traveled quickly, separating near the Mississippi River. When Laura rode into thick woods she became fearful, especially when she saw a man approaching her. When he drew closer, the man pulled up and looked at her curiously.

"I wonder if you are not the woman I am looking for," he said. All fear left her when she noticed the man's physical resemblance to another man she knew.

"I believe you are the man I am looking for," she replied evenly. The man was Brother Follett's son. He was carrying a note from Morris which he had meant to deliver to Laura, as they feared she might now be in jail.

Turning about, they began their journey home, arriving in Quincey the following day. Morris was much recovered in mind and body. He was overjoyed to see his brave wife who had risked so much on his behalf. Reunited at last, Morris and Laura left to join their children in Iowa.

Upon Laura Phelp's death at age thirty-six, in 1842, the Prophet Joseph Smith spoke of her courage. He said,

"She was driven from Jackson County in 1833, was in the persecution of Missouri in 1838, and went from Iowa to Missouri to assist in liberating her husband, and was left in the prison yard when he made his escape, willing to suffer all the abuses a savage horde could inflict upon her to set her companion free from the grasp of his murderous enemies. Her rest is glorious."

# 20

## "Our Baby Is Back There Alone!"

Marn Peterson

Sister Marn Peterson was making the long trek to the Salt Lake Valley with her husband Oli and their baby girl Annie when dysentery struck the company. This new disaster came during a desperate time when the pioneers were hurrying to get through hostile Indian territory. Marn became anxious when her little daughter Annie contracted the disease and became seriously ill. The baby's condition worsened until her life was hanging by a thread. Finally, the distraught parents called for the company leader who, when he examined Annie, found that the spark of life had gone out.

"Your baby has been called home," he told them gently, then tried to offer comfort by reminding them, "The Lord giveth and the Lord taketh away." But his next words stunned them into agonized despair.

"We haven't time to dig a grave. We have delayed too long now. Besides, if the Indians found a newly-dug grave they would know how recently we have passed here and follow us. Wrap your baby in a blanket and place her under this bush so she cannot be seen, and hurry along."

Although their hearts were broken at losing their precious little girl, the parents obeyed, and the company continued its journey. That evening, members of the group tried to console the bereaved parents, who were doubly sorrowful because they had earlier lost a newborn son. Once again, the familiar strains of "Come, Come Ye Saints," echoed across the prairie. But instead of feeling comforted, Marn felt as if her heart was torn apart. She could not join in the singing.

As the evening wore on, the pioneers retired one by one to their beds. Still grieving, Marn and Oli remained by the flickering campfire. Suddenly Marn burst out, "Oli, I can't feel that our baby was dead!"

"I know dear," her husband replied sorrowfully, "we had so many plans. But she was and there is nothing we can do about it but pray that we will be able to raise a family when we settle in Zion. So go to the wagon so you will be refreshed for tomorrow's travel." Slowly, Marn arose and walked wearily to their wagon. Suddenly, the eerie howling of wolves pierced the chill night air. She stopped in her tracks.

"Oli!" she wailed, "Listen to those wolves, and our baby is lying back there all alone, not even a grave for protection! How can we stand to go on?" Resolutely he replied, "We must make up our minds to go and trust in the Lord for the rest."

"I can't, I can't," she moaned. Gently, Oli held her a moment before helping her to their wagon and the blessed relief of sleep.

When Oli woke with the dawn he turned to his wife's place beside him. It was empty! He sprang up and hurried outside and looked around the wagons. She was nowhere to be found. Fear clutched his heart as he asked other early risers if they had seen Marn. Nobody had.

F THOMAS 99

His mind was whirling with panic as he organized the Saints into search parties. What could have happened to Marn? Perhaps Indians had captured her, or maybe she had fallen victim to wild beasts, he thought. But the thing that puzzled him most was why Marn, a timid woman, would go out alone into the dangerous prairie that she greatly feared.

Hour after anxious hour passed. Glumly, the search parties returned without the missing woman and plans were made to continue the journey.

Suddenly someone shouted, "There she comes!" Oli looked down the long trail they had traveled the day before and saw his wife stumbling along the dirt trail, clutching a bundle tightly to her chest. It was her blanket-wrapped baby. Relief flooded over Oli as he ran down the trail to his wife. Despite his overpowering relief, he gently chided her.

"Darling, why didn't you wake me and tell me you were going back to the baby?" He didn't wait for an answer, but carefully took the blanket-wrapped child from her arms. He started, then looked at Marn with unbelieving eyes.

"Our baby, she's warm!" he exclaimed. "She isn't stiff and cold like dead babies are!" He flung back the covers to stare at his precious child, then shouted with unbelievable joy, "She's alive!"

The Saints gathered and reached out eager hands to feel the baby and witness the miracle. The company leader came over and viewed the baby. It was weak from hunger and exposure but definitely alive.

"Brother Peterson," he solemnly stated, "I was positive your baby was dead yesterday, but she is alive now. Her sojourn here has not been completed. May God's choicest blessings descend upon her and help her to live and to finish her mission on earth."

# 21

## *She Threw Away the Gunstocks*

Abigail Leonard

On July 3rd, 1832, Abigail Leonard and other Saints started for Jackson County, Missouri. They arrived in December and lived in peace until persecutions began in the spring of 1833. Matters worsened; then a crisis occurred when a mob attacked a group of unarmed Mormon men in the woods. One of them managed to break away and go for help, and Abigail's husband was among those who responded to his plea.

A group of men hurried the six miles to the forest to defend their brothers and were eventually able to defeat the mob. Brother Leonard returned home dirty and bedraggled. Although Abigail counted fourteen bullet holes in his clothes, she could find no wounds on him except two slight marks on his hip and arm.

After that battle, the brethren signed a treaty with the mob, stating that if they would stop their attacks, the Saints would leave the area. Thus began the exodus of the Saints from Jackson County into Clay County, Missouri. However, their arrival alarmed the inhabitants of Clay County so badly that in a desperate attempt to stop the influx of Mormons, they cut away the ferry boat, leaving Abigail and nine other families stranded in Jackson County.

Even though they had no way to cross the Missouri River, the mob insisted that those left behind were in violation of the treaty. So on November 13th, 1833, the mob forced them out into the desolate prairie at bayonet point. The families spent the first cold night without shelter of any kind. The next day, they were forced to march on even though many of them were barefoot. The ground had red imprints from their bleeding feet as they walked over the barren ground. The Leonard family were the only ones with shoes and socks. Abigail asked the Lord what she should do and said, "His answer was; 'Divide among the sufferers and thou shalt be repaid four-fold!' I then gave till I had given more than fifteen pairs of stockings."

The group traveled for three and a half days, finally making camp for the duration of the winter in a grove of trees near a stream. They managed to survive only because the mob periodically allowed the men to return to their homes to get needed supplies.

Then came word that they would not be allowed to return for any more provisions. The Saints tried to buy food from the local people, but they refused to sell any provisions, leaving the Saints with two options: sit and starve in the forest or return to Jackson County.

Abigail and her family returned home late on the evening of February 20th, 1934. A few days after their return, they were sitting before a blazing fire, enjoying the welcome warmth from their Dutch fireplace, when they heard a slight noise outside. A friend went out and returned shortly with the dreadful news that a mob had been seen nearby. At that moment, it was riding hard toward the house. The children began crying with fear and raced outside to hide.

Abigail said, "In a moment or two, five armed men pushed their way into the house and presented their guns to my husband's breast and demanded, 'Are you a Mormon?'"

"I profess to belong to the Church of Christ," he bravely replied. When asked if there were any guns in the house, the Leonards assured them they didn't have any weapons.

The men commanded him to walk outside, but Brother Leonard refused to budge. In a fury, one of the men laid down his gun, grabbed a chair, and smashed it upon his head. Fortunately, as he swung the chair above him in an arc, it hit a beam overhead which softened the blow. Brother Leonard remained standing, but the chair was smashed to bits.

Abigail relates what happened next. "The fiend then caught another chair, with which he succeeded in knocking my husband down beneath the stairway. They then struck him several blows with a chair post upon the head, cutting four long gashes in the scalp." Sister Leonard begged for mercy and tried to go to her husband's rescue, but the other men held her back.

Two men grabbed Brother Leonard's feet and after dragging him into another room, stood him upright. Two men stayed close beside him to make sure he didn't fall while he swayed on his feet. Then a mobster got a huge rock and, as Abigail watched in horror, threw it with all of his might at her husband's head. Dazed as he was, Brother Leonard saw it coming and ducked just in time. It sailed harmlessly through the room, where it crashed heavily against the wall. Abigail stated later that it "went against the house like a cannonball."

Two of the mobbers then grabbed Brother Leonard. Lifting him mightily into the air, they released him, letting him crash heavily upon the ground. One of the men then jumped upon the bleeding man's chest, breaking two of his ribs as he stomped. Not yet finished, the men rolled Brother Leonard onto his side and began using a chair post to try to break his thigh. His wife stated that the blows could be heard at a distance of 120 rods (700 yards).

The mob then took her husband outside, where they stripped off his coat and shirt, preparing him for further torture. No longer held back by the mob, Sister Leonard followed them outside, unwilling to leave her husband despite the danger to herself.

"Take that woman in the house," one of the gunmen shouted, "or she will overpower every devil of you!" Jumping up and pointing their guns at her, four men yelled and cursed as they ordered Sister Leonard back into the house. But she stood her ground, stoutly refusing to leave her husband alone.

When the merciless mob began beating the nearly unconscious man with their gunstocks, something inside Abigail snapped. Rushing into the middle of the mob, she began snatching the gunstocks out of the men's hands, heaving each one as far away as her strength would allow. Stunned, the men looked upon the outraged woman incredulously. Not one man lifted a hand to stop her as she threw away at least twenty gunstocks.

Despite her heroic actions, it looked as if her efforts were in vain. At that moment, Brother Leonard felt that he could not live a minute longer. Raising trembling hands to the heavens, he asked the Lord to receive his spirit, then closed his eyes.

The mobbers stood silently by as Abigail screamed frantically for help from a woman who had remained hidden in the house. Together, the women managed to carry Brother Leonard into the house. He was alive, though unconscious. Carefully they washed his bruised

F THOMAS 99

and bloodied body and tended to his wounds. From time to time, Abigail glanced out the window at the mob who were still milling about in the yard. She wondered if they were waiting to see if he was dead and worried that they might come back inside and try to finish their job. The idea left her shaken.

When she had made her husband as comfortable as possible, Abigail prayed for inspiration on what to do. Then, rising to her feet, she bravely strode outside, silently asking for the Spirit to continue to guide her. The mob who had come so close to murdering her husband gathered round her. Abigail talked to them for a minute, then asked if her husband had ever harmed any one of them. There was complete silence.

She pointed out that in spite of the terrible beating he had just received, her husband had not once raised an arm to defend himself. The men's roughened faces softened slightly and Abigail grew hopeful. She continued to speak as the men shuffled around, glancing furtively at each other.

Finally, one of the men drifted away and the rest followed his lead, quietly leaving. When they were out of sight, Abigail quickly sent for two brethren, and they gave her husband a priesthood blessing. Instantly, his condition improved. He continued to regain his strength at an amazing rate all that afternoon and evening. Even the deep cuts on his head grew together and in time there was not even a scar left.

The next day was Sunday and Brother Leonard felt so well that he insisted on attending his meetings with his brave and spirited wife Abigail. He still marveled at how his wife had defied the hardened mob to save his life.

# 22

## She Would Not Leave Him

### Drusilla Hendricks

Near Far West, 1837, tensions were running high. The Saints became anxious and fearful as people in the area started rising up against them. When the Saints were told they had to give up their land that had been lawfully purchased, they refused. They prepared to defend themselves as mobs gathered to force them to leave.

A group of 25–30 brethren met to discuss the situation, gathering upstairs at the Hendricks home. Drusilla said that "soon after, I had to go upstairs for something and . . . was very frightened and found the bed full of guns, pistols, and swords."

In the end, the Hendricks and others gave up their land without a fight and moved on to Caldwell County. They built a cabin and raised hay. Too soon, the situation there also turned tense. One evening, they looked out to see the prairie on fire, the wind driving the flames directly toward them. James and Drusilla went out to fight the fire but there wasn't time to back light it. Instead they were forced to run for their lives. Twelve tons of their stacked hay was burned, though they managed to save the house.

As the months went by, Drusilla's life followed a regular cycle: her family would begin to prosper in one place, just to have to move again when anti-Mormon sentiment rose too high. After Drusilla had her fifth child in March, 1838, trouble began again in their new home.

James spent much of his time standing guard to protect the Saints. He was on call at all hours of the day or night. When he heard the prearranged signal of three taps of the drum, he was to go out and help defend their little community. Ofttimes when he was summoned, Drusilla and the children would weep with worry. Although she did her best to gather in their crops with the help of her children, much was destroyed while James was on duty.

Drusilla said that on October 24th, 1838, "the mob gathered on the south of us and sent out the word that they would burn everything they came to and that they already had two of our brethren as prisoners and the prairies were black with smoke."

One afternoon, a group of men, among them Joseph and Hyrum Smith, came to Drusilla's back door to reassure her. They told her they thought the mob was burning the grass and outer houses to frighten the inhabitants into leaving so they could rob and plunder the empty homes.

That evening, James and his wife went outside. When Drusilla noticed his erect form ahead of her in the still night air, she said, "The thought came to me that I might never see him so straight and erect again."

After prayer, they fell asleep exhausted. Drusilla had a dream that something terrible had befallen her husband. She had just gathered him in her arms when Brother Charles Rich knocked at the door, waking them, saying James was needed. Drusilla laid a fire and got her husband's overcoat, tucking his pistols in the pockets. Then she got his sword and, after belting it snugly around him, bid him good-bye and watched him ride off.

The next morning, October 25th, was spent in anxious waiting. In the afternoon a neighbor child came over and told the Hendricks children that their father had been shot. Drusilla ran out into the field and sobbed out her fears in private. When she was done, Drusilla said, "I went back to the house and found the children all crying. I went to the loom to try and weave to let on to them that I did not believe the report about their father. I could not weave at all."

Drusilla sat motionless until a rider reined up outside. Running out, Drusilla recognized him as a friend, Mr. T. Snider. When he told her James had been shot through the hip, Drusilla left her children in the care of a woman who lived with them and rode four miles to reach her husband. James was lying cold and motionless on a bed. He had not been shot in the hip, but in the neck and was paralyzed from the neck down. Although he could speak, he could not move anymore than if he was dead. Three other injured men lay in the house, one of them David W. Patten, a member of the Twelve Apostles.

"It is of no use for me to try and tell how I felt," Drusilla stated later, "for that is impossible, but I could not have shed a tear if all had been dead before me. I went to work to try and get my husband warm but could not." However, she continued to try to rub some warmth into his cold body.

At dusk, a neighbor came with a wagon and bed and took James and Drusilla to Far West. They stayed there, while neighbors cared for their children at home, until the Saints surrendered. When they returned to their house, they found the mob had robbed it of bedding, utensils, crockery—everything, in fact, except the beds.

James was still unable to move hand or foot. So it was left to Drusilla to settle business matters and make arrangements for them to get out of the state. She arranged to sell what she could and traded their land for a small sum of money and two yoke of cattle. They left everything behind except a few things that could be put into a small wagon. They moved once again, settling temporarily in a tiny cabin.

In the middle of January, 1839, Joseph Smith Senior and Isaac Morley, with five or six others, anointed and administered to James. Then they stood him on his feet and worked his shoulders, which seemed to have a good effect. Meanwhile, Drusilla continued to nurse him, rubbing him with strong vinegar, salt, and liniments.

The Mormons were leaving the area as fast as they could. But Drusilla didn't know how they could until Brother Isaac Leaney, a man who had been wounded at Haun's Mill, told her not to worry. He said he would see to it that her family was not left behind. Drusilla said, "He had been shot through and through from both sides, the balls passing through the lungs, but he was miraculously healed. He had twenty-seven bullet holes in his shirt. I counted them myself. He only had eleven wounds to be dressed."

Then, one night the dog began barking. Drusilla's oldest son, William, peeked outside. "Mother," he whispered, agitated, "the mob is coming." Soon she could hear them swearing at the dog as they crossed the yard to their cabin. They tried to open the door. Finding it fastened shut, they yelled at her to open the door or they would break it. When she opened it, she was disconcerted to see that one of the men had a large bowie knife in one hand and a pistol in the other.

Turning abruptly, Drusilla hurried back to sit upon her husband's bed. But the men crossed the room to where the helpless man lay and ordered her to get up. Though she was shaking with fright, she refused, feeling she was the only protection her husband had. Adamantly, she told them that she was watching James and would not move. The men picked up a candle and held it over her pallid husband to see better, then turned down his bed clothes and asked what doctor she was using.

"I have none," she replied. They asked many more questions, then said they wanted to search the house. One of them handed his pistol to the other and took the candle. The other man told Drusilla to get up so he could look under the bed. But she would only move an inch or two higher on the bed.

She suddenly remembered a dream she had three months earlier. In the dream, her husband was lying sick on the bed, nearly dead, when two men came in with the intention of killing him if they could get him alone. In her dream, she had told them they would have to kill her first. These mobbers matched the men in her dream so closely that she was more determined than ever to stay and guard James.

The other man came back from his short search and together they looked under the bed. They told her they were looking for Stephen Winchester.

"Go to Illinois if you want to find him," Drusilla said tartly.

"His wife has been telling us that lie, but we don't believe it," they answered. She told them the date Brother Winchester had left. But they continued to explore, looking under the rest of the beds at the back of the house.

Finding nothing, they came to stand beside Drusilla, eyeing her husband suspiciously. She kept a close watch on their weapons. She said later, "I sat still on the side of the bed for I was determined I would not leave him.

F THOMAS

They made him talk, but he was so weak and pale, he looked more like he was dead than alive."

The men asked Drusilla for water but she refused to get it. "There is a cup and a pail over there, but you can get it for I will not get up," she said, pointing toward the table. She felt that she must stay at her husband's side to safeguard him, though she endangered her life by angering the intruders. After drinking their fill, they sat beside the pile of wood that had been brought in for the night. They began putting powder in their pistols while Drusilla sat nervously, wondering what they intended.

One man finally spoke up. "All is ready." Each man put his finger on the trigger of his pistol and slowly arose. Drusilla held her breath, fully expecting them to fire their guns at James or herself. They stood motionless for a long minute before suddenly slinking out the door without another word.

Although Drusilla had managed to protect her husband, she still faced the problem of how to move her family out of danger while he remained so helpless. The Saints were leaving as fast as they could, while the mob continued to threaten those left behind.

Drusilla could not make the move while her husband was in such poor condition but began making arrangements for future travel. As the months passed, Drusilla spent endless hours nursing her husband and taking care of her children, trying not to let the mobbers terrorize her. Taking care of her husband was physically draining. She said, "I had to lift him at least fifty times a day and in doing so I had to strain every nerve."

Through the power of priesthood blessings and dedicated nursing, James' condition improved so that he was finally able to stand. In March, Brother Leaney fulfilled his promise and brought a yoke of cattle to the

Hendricks's door. After helping them load their belongings, he saw them on to Quincy, Illinois. It was now March, 1839.

After their arrival, the local brethren secured a bottle of oil and consecrated it. With Joseph Smith Senior at the head, they sat James on a chair and anointed and administered to him once more. They then assisted Brother Hendricks to his feet. He walked a distance of thirty yards, with two men on either side of him for support.

Their new quarters in Quincy were partly underground, with poor air circulation. James became ill and bedridden once more. In order to buy food, Drusilla hired out her cattle, saving only one for the little milk it provided. But when a mob drove the cattle off, that little income was gone. A new trial struck the family when James became stricken with a terrible affliction.

"Like Job of old," Drusilla stated, "he broke [out] in sores all over his body so that you could not put a pin point on him without putting it on a sore, from the crown of his head to the soles of his feet."

During this time, Drusilla ran out of bread and meat. She stated, "We had one spoonful of sugar and one saucerful of corn meal so I made mush of the meal and put the sugar on it and gave it to my children." Having no food whatsoever in the house, and being burdened with an invalid husband, Drusilla thought about all the trials she had been through. She remembered her parents' dire warnings against becoming a member of the Church. Then she decided, "I did what was right, if I die, I am glad I was baptized."

That afternoon, a friend, Rubin Alred, came and asked if she had bread. When she replied they had none, Rubin said he'd had a feeling they didn't. He went back to his wagon and got a sack of meal, which he gave to Sister Hendricks.

Through Drusilla's courage, faith, and diligent nursing, James partly recovered. However, he remained an invalid the rest of his life. The Hendrickses continued to move with the main body of Saints. When Brigham Young told the Saints the time had come to go west, Drusilla courageously made arrangements so that her family could cross the plains with the other pioneers. After their arrival in the Rocky Mountains, they made their home in Salt Lake City.

# 23

## "God Rules!"

Lydia Knight

As Joseph Smith had baptized Lydia into the Church, it seemed fitting that he should perform her marriage ceremony two years later. Apparently, this was the first marriage ceremony the Prophet had ever performed. Because it was a punishable offense for a layman to officiate at a wedding, and because Ohio did not recognize Mormon elders as ministers, most did not perform marriages. However, on November 23rd , 1835, Joseph felt inspired to use his authority on Lydia's behalf. He declared afterwards that from that time forth he would perform marriage ceremonies whenever he saw fit.

Fair-haired Lydia and her husband Newel made their home in Far West, a lovely little town with rich fields, comfortable houses, and barns. However, the local people were disturbed at the presence of the Saints and began threatening them.

During the August election, the Saints were explicitly warned not to think of voting. The few that did go to the polls were roughly assaulted, though they were successful in casting their votes. Their determination to cast their ballots further angered the local people. They began to organize into mobs to plunder the Saints' fields, drive off their stock, and in some cases attack the people.

About mid-October, word went out that a mob had assembled at a little settlement on Crooked River. The Mormon militia organized themselves but in the ensuing battle were defeated. A few days later, a messenger brought the news that a great multitude of the enemy was camped outside the city, intent on razing the town to the ground. Lydia spent the night hiding her household goods so they wouldn't be destroyed should the mob carry out its threats.

Before Newel left that night to stand guard, he told his wife, "My dear, be careful of our little ones tonight. I must go out and join my brethren who are on guard. You will not be afraid will you?"

"Newel, God rules!" Lydia replied bravely, resolving to leave the matter in more capable hands.

She had cause to be afraid, however. Later, two frightened and desperate brethren came to her door, begging for help. One of them, James Emmet, was a friend of Lydia's. He asked if she would hide them from the mob, which was searching for them. The mob had sworn to murder any man who had taken part in the Battle of Crooked River, and both of them had fought there. Though she was putting her own life in peril, Lydia quickly pulled them inside. She told them she would do everything in her power to keep them safe.

That night, she worked busily fashioning a little storage room adjoining the living room into a hiding place, making it as comfortable as she could for the two fugitives. When morning came, she dressed her children and tried to go about her daily routine. She knew the mob would likely kill her, and perhaps the children also, if they found out she had hidden the two men in her house.

She bolstered her courage by repeating to herself, "God rules!"

Lydia spent the day in work and prayer, many times dropping to her knees to plead for the safety of her children and the brethren she was concealing. Later in the day, a neighbor came to her house to tell her the Prophet Joseph had gone to the enemy camp under a flag of truce to see if he could do something about the extermination order.

When she found out Lydia knew nothing about the infamous order, the neighbor clucked her tongue and said, "Well, you must have stayed close at home last night not to have heard that!"

"Yes," Lydia replied wryly, without disclosing her dangerous secret. "I was very busy all night."

Not long after the woman had gone, the air was broken with shouts from the camp of the mob. When Lydia looked anxiously from the window, she saw her husband running to the house. He told her Joseph had been betrayed and taken prisoner.

"Do not go outside the house," he warned her. "Prowlers are around and will injure you if they find you in their power. I must go now, my girl. . . . Be brave as you always are."

"Be careful, my husband," Lydia begged him, then added stoutly, "I feel that we shall be protected."

Once more Lydia was left alone with her secret. She continued to care for her household. When apprehensions began to overcome her, she prayed for strength. Several times, she felt the Spirit whisper in answer to her worries, "Be still!"

Throughout the night, she could hear awful shouts and shrieks from the mob. She trembled to know whether her friend, the Prophet Joseph, was still in their hands. She spent the night in a series of long, concerned prayers.

The next morning, November 1st, dawned cool and bright, and with it came Newel. He gave her the latest news. All men were ordered to surrender. Too soon, he had to leave again. "Goodbye and God protect you," Newel said tightly. "I must go, for there is the signal for us to gather at the public square."

Snatching his rifle from the wall, he rushed off. But once Newel had joined his brethren at the square, General Lucas demanded that the men give up their weapons or be shot on the spot. They had no choice but to comply. After they were disarmed and placed under guard, the mob began swarming into the town to loot, ravish, and demolish with no one to stop them. Cattle were shot, fields were destroyed, women were attacked, and homes were invaded, the mobbers taking anything of value.

Every home was searched in an effort to uncover any men who had been at the Battle of Crooked River. Three of the mob came to Lydia's house.

"Have you any men in the house?" the leader asked.

"You have our men under guard," was Lydia's shrewd reply.

Not satisfied with that response, he repeated his question impatiently. "Have you any man in the house?"

"I tell you," Lydia replied with a touch of sharpness in her voice, "my husband is on the public square as a prisoner." He decided to try a different tactic.

"Have you any arms in the house?"

"My husband took his rifle with him," Lydia answered amidst whimpers as her children began to cry, frightened at the rough strangers. "Sir," she begged the man, concern showing in her light blue eyes, "go away from here, do you not see how frightened my little ones are?"

"Well, have you no men or arms in the house?"

"I tell you again, my husband is a prisoner on the square and he took his rifle with him." With one last coarse comment, the men turned away, miraculously leaving the house without the thorough search that others had been subject too.

"God rules!" a trembling mother whispered to her children. Lydia kept the men hidden again one more night, after which they were able to flee to safety.

The next morning, the sun rose on the desolation of the town. She came out of her house to see hundreds of homeless people huddled together because their houses had been destroyed by the mob. Lydia was one of the fortunate few to have her home intact. She, together with the few others who had been spared, shared their food with those who had none.

The mob held a mock trial. The Mormon prisoners were tried without being permitted to be present and without any type of defense. When General Doniphan heard that the Mormons were sentenced to be shot, he told his fellow soldiers he would have nothing to do with such unlawful proceedings and left in disgust.

The mob then had a change of heart and decided to move Joseph Smith, Amasa Lyman, Sidney Rigdon, Parley P. Pratt, Lyman Wight, and George W. Robinson to Independence. They told the rest of the Saints they were free but had just a few months to get out of the area.

Lydia and Newel were in a dilemma about how to move. The mob had killed all their stock except for one cow. Finally, they managed to find a man who would take them to the Mississippi River in exchange for that animal.

Hasty preparations were made. In the cold of winter, with snow piled so high it sometimes reached the hubs of the wagon, they left on their journey of several hundred miles. Often, they had to scrape the snow away in the evening to make their beds. The nights were intensely cold. Detained in their travels, they didn't reach the river until May 1st.

Once across the Mississippi, Lydia noted the low marshy plain that was covered with grass and stretched for miles. Here and there, a few belts of timber relieved the monotony of the landscape. This small settlement was to be the beginning of "Nauvoo the Beautiful."

A few houses were scattered about in the area. Mostly, there were tents, bush wickiups, and crude shelters of every description. Lydia and her family sewed some of their bedclothes together to form a rude tent. The grass was green but damp. Water was plentiful but warm, an ideal breeding ground for sickness.

It took only a few weeks before people began to see how deadly the air rising from the swamps and marshes could be. First to become ill were the infirm and aged. Then, diseases began attacking children. Fevers of all kinds became prevalent. Even those who had been strong succumbed to disease.

People began dying, and there were not enough healthy bodies to bury them. Pestilence and fever were at every fireside. Even the Prophet Joseph, who had escaped from his enemies in Independence, was stricken. His yard was filled with the sick and dying who had come hoping to be healed by their leader. Finally, Joseph regained some strength and began going about tending to the sick with his wife, Emma. Hundreds were healed by his hand.

During this trying year of 1839, Lydia, whose health was not good, had gone about the area ministering to others. She not only tended her own ailing household but helped those around her who were stricken. Though pale and weak, Lydia nursed the Saints until September.

Her body, worn out with heavy labor, succumbed to the disease. For several days and nights, she lay sweltering with a burning fever.

"Newel," she whispered to her husband, "go and ask the Prophet to send me a handkerchief with his blessing."

Newel hesitated. "My dear wife," he said reluctantly, "I do not like to trouble Joseph. You have no idea how worn down he is. He has asked the brethren to spare him as much as possible, for these constant, never-ceasing calls upon him are depriving him of all his strength."

Lydia desisted. But after an agonizing night and morning, she again asked her husband to go to the Prophet and get a handkerchief with his blessing. Newel went out and after some time returned with the cloth, which he tied over her head, saying, "There, Lydia, is a handkerchief."

However, Lydia felt no relief and even grew worse. A doctor was brought in, but his efforts were in vain. A few days later, Lydia felt her time on earth was near its end. She tried to speak to her husband but could only manage a faint whisper.

"Newel, I am all but done with my suffering; goodbye dear one. You must do the best you can with the children. I cannot last much longer." After listening to her broken whisper, Newel hurried away. When he returned, she recognized him but was unable to speak.

"Here, Lydia," he bent over her, whispering contritely, "here is a handkerchief from the Prophet Joseph. Oh my wife, the one I brought before was not from him, I so hated to trouble him. But see, this is from Joseph and he says your Heavenly Father shall heal you and you shall be restored to life and health."

With those words, he tied the handkerchief around her head and the blessing that was contained within entered her body. She closed her eyelids in quiet slumber. During the night she awoke, astonished at how much better she felt. In the morning, the doctor came again.

"Why, I never saw such a change in my life!" he exclaimed joyfully. "That last medicine has worked like a charm. I wish I'd stayed and seen it operate." He turned to Newel in amazement. "Her pulse is all right, her tongue is all right, and in fact she is comparatively a well woman." Newel hated to burst the doctor's bubble but quietly reached up and pulled the doctor's bottle of medicine from the shelf. It was full.

"Sir, there is the medicine you speak of. My wife has not tasted one drop of it."

"But what's the meaning of all this change then?"

"She has been healed by faith through the Prophet Joseph Smith." Although he was not a Mormon, the doctor was pleased that the ill woman was doing better.

"Well," he commented graciously, "it's a good thing to get well on any terms."

That day, Lydia got up, dressed, and began tending to her household once more. As she did before her illness, she spent most of her time nursing others and was especially concerned about her baby, James, who was very ill. Newel became stricken, as well as his niece Harriet, who lived with them. Lydia remained busy taking care of them all. Once in a while, neighbors came to help. But they chided Lydia, feeling she was clinging too much to her baby.

"Let him go," they told her. "Give him up, and his sufferings will be at an end."

"Oh, I cannot think of such a thing," replied the loving mother. "Father Smith said in my blessing that my heart should not be pained because of the loss of my children . . . I feel that it is not the Lord's will that I should part with him."

The next Sunday, the child looked more like a skeleton than anything. He was barely breathing, his skin was drawn, and his eyes were glassy. In a panic, Lydia beseeched Newel to tell her what more she could do than what she had already done.

"You can do no more," Newel conceded. "Give him up and ask God to soften this great blow to us both."

"It is impossible," Lydia cried fervently. "I cannot give him up." That night she watched him closely. Early the next morning, the Prophet happened to be passing their house when Lydia glanced out the window. Running outside, she begged him to come in and see her baby. Although he was shocked at the baby's appearance, he looked deeply into Lydia's determined eyes as she insisted she would not stop trying to save him.

He paused a moment in thought, then smiled gently. "Sister Lydia, I do not think you will have to give him up." He told her to have another brother come and administer in a certain way to the baby. She did so immediately and the baby revived somewhat. However, a week later he suffered a relapse. After many anxious hours, she again followed Joseph's advice and had two brethren come and repeat the blessing.

As the elders' hands rested upon the baby's little head, a light shone down upon the child, a solitary brilliant sunbeam from a cloudy sky. When they finished speaking, the light faded and the child immediately began to improve. His renewed health was a tribute and testimony to a faithful and courageous mother.

# 24

# She Helped Her Husband Escape

Sarah Rich

As mobs made sweeping raids through the countryside near Far West, Missouri, the Saints were forced to gather together for protection. Fleeing from persecutors, Sarah Pea Rich and her husband, Charles C. Rich, left their home and traveled to the home of Sarah's parents, which lay vacant. Others, such as John E. Page, one of the Twelve Apostles, and Charles's sister Samantha and her husband, Hosea Stout, were not so fortunate in finding shelter.

Sarah said of that time, "I took in seven families. Among that number was John E. Page and his wife. One week after, his wife died and as the mob was troubling us so severely at this time, it was impossible to have Sister Page buried for three days."

Finally, the brethren tried once again to make peace with their enemies. A small group went to the nearby mob's camp with Charles carrying a white flag of truce. When the men arrived at the camp, they met with one of the leaders, a preacher named Samuel Bogart. He was surprised to see Charles and recognized him as one of the Mormons who had been at the recent Battle of Crooked River. David W. Patten, one of the Twelve Apostles, had been mortally wounded in that battle and

Charles had knelt and administered to Elder Patten before taking over as commander.

Bogart was full of hatred toward all Mormons and, since the battle, toward Charles in particular. Their attempt to negotiate peace was fruitless. The brethren started to leave. As Charles turned away, however, still carrying the flag of truce, his back provided too tempting a target for Bogart. He fired, narrowly missing Charles' broad shoulders. Sarah stood anxiously at her doorway.

"I saw them shoot at him while bearing a white flag with a message from our people to them in order to try and make peace." The brethren fled, while the mob began vowing to kill them.

Charles raced to the public square to hide briefly at his sister's home, which was above the store she and her husband owned. Sarah, who was seven months pregnant, met her husband there together with her in-laws, Hosea and Samantha. Hastily, they made plans for the men to escape.

Sarah was especially fearful for her husband's safety. Charles was a tall and large man who was well known because of his prominence in the Church. She was aware the mob would be looking specifically for him. Because of his size, it would be nearly impossible for him to effect a disguise. They made plans for Charles and Hosea to leave as soon as the protective cloak of darkness had fallen.

That evening, Sarah and Charles found it difficult to part. They had been married less than a year and each was fearful for the other's safety. They wondered if they would ever see one another again. To ease their minds, the couple devised a plan that would help protect them. Sarah explained this in her journal:

> Him (Charles) and Hosea Stout made a covenant to stay together until we should meet again and Hosey's wife

> and I made a covenant that her and I would remain together as true friends until we should meet our husbands again and upon this promise we shook hands with our dear husbands and parted. Her and I then went into my sister-in-laws house and went to bed praying the Lord to protect ourselves and our dear companions until He saw fit to have us meet again.

When morning came, Sarah and Samantha left the store and were nearing Sarah's home when they ran into a roadblock. The men guarding the road refused to let the women pass, even when Sarah explained they were simply going home. Picking up their skirts, they attempted to pass but the guards swung pointed bayonets at them and ordered them back. Tired after a sleepless night spent worrying about her husband, Sarah felt dejected at having to turn back. Samantha, who was ill from a lingering disease, was equally discouraged.

Returning to the store, they related their experience to Sarah's sister-in-law. They were overheard by a man in the back of the store, who asked about their problem. Not knowing who he was, Sarah said she couldn't get through to her home because rough guards were blocking the road. The man then identified himself as the captain of the guards, and Sarah's wan face grew even paler. She was quaking when he asked a question that sent her mind reeling.

"Was it your husband that Captain Beauregarde killed yesterday?"

Sarah sat stunned, still trying to take in the fact that she had been talking to the enemy. Her quick mind soon realized, however, that this bit of rumor, if it were believed, could be used to protect her beloved husband. After all, she quickly deduced, if the mob thought Charles was dead, they would call off the manhunt, allowing him to escape.

F THOMAS

Sarah knew that if she acknowledged the death of her husband, she could provide Charles with the time he needed to elude those who wanted to kill him. Though it could be dangerous for her once the truth was discovered, she didn't hesitate to speak the words that could help save her husband's life.

Sarah looked up at the captain and replied that what he heard was true. The captain took pity on the new widow, so heavily pregnant, and on her ill friend, and offered to accompany them home.

As they walked down the road, Sarah told him of other troubles. A few days ago, she had sent her hired boy out with a team of oxen to get a load of firewood. Mobbers had taken the boy prisoner and kept the oxen. The captain asked for the name of the boy and a description of the cattle, assuring her that he would see to it the boy was released and the oxen returned.

Reaching the guards, the captain ordered them to stand aside. Sarah and Samantha passed by gratefully. When the women neared her home, Sarah was surprised to see two men standing near her team of oxen in front of the house. At that moment, the men raised their guns and Sarah realized in horror they were about to shoot her animals.

The captain shouted at the men just in time to hold their fire. He then called a man over and told him to go to the prisoner camp and release Sarah's hired boy. Next, he ordered men to hitch up the team of oxen and fetch a load of wood so the exhausted women would have a good supply. Grateful for the unexpected help, the women took charge again of the house.

Unfortunately, the many kindnesses shown by the captain were but the lull before the storm. Sarah heard no further word of her husband but felt assured he had managed to escape. She wrote, "His [the captain of the guard] carrying the impression into camp that my husband was killed, kept it [the mob] from looking for him until he had time to get out of the way."

However, the time came when Sarah's lie was discovered. News of her husband's activities finally reached the mob. When they learned that Charles Rich still lived, they immediately stormed Sarah's home, furious at her deception. Sarah recorded the following in her journal:

> When they (the mob) found out he was not killed they felt awful mad and would often come to my house and tell me if I did not tell where he was hid they would blow my brains out, at the same time pointing pistols at me. For they thought he must be hid up some where, never once thinking it possible for him to make his escape when there was so many troops of mobs in the country.

Several times, the mob threatened to burn the house. They stole the expensive horse her father had given her earlier that year. They took her chickens and drove off the cows that had given the women much-needed milk. The continued uproar took its toll on the women's health, leaving them ill and weak.

Sarah endured nearly three months of persecution until her father arrived to take the women to their husbands. Sarah and Samantha, both feeling very sick, packed their belongings. With the help of Sarah's brother-in-law, Thomas Rich, they left in two wagons during the cold of February.

Sarah was so ill during the four-hundred-mile journey that she had to lie prone in the wagon most of the time. As she was near giving birth, Thomas was required to help her in and out of the wagon night and morning. Finally, they reached the banks of the Mississippi across which lay the city of Quincy. The women knew their husbands were on the other side, but between them and their husbands lay the dangerous, ice-filled river. Crowded around them were other Saints waiting to cross.

When George D. Grant saw how downcast the women were, he made an effort to cheer them up by telling them he would go across the river and tell Charles and Hosea of their arrival. He set off at once, but as he neared the opposite side the ice broke, and he fell into the freezing river. Fortunately, Charles and Hosea were close by and came to his rescue. When they found out their beloved wives were so close, they were determined to cross the river.

The men obtained a skiff. Carrying it across the frozen ice to where the water was running, they jumped in and came down the river. Sarah was ecstatic. "Great was our joy to meet with our dear companions who were compelled to part with us three months before and flee for their lives from a howling mob."

The women crossed the dangerous river with their husbands and arrived safely in Quincy. Shortly after, Sarah had her baby. With her new infant in her arms and her husband at her side, Sarah could feel nothing but satisfaction at the sacrifice that had helped save the life of her husband.

# Bibliographical References


| Hero/Heroine | Chapter | Reference |
|---|---|---|
| Berg, Anna | 4 | Kris Mackay, *The Outstretched Arms* (Salt Lake City: Bookcraft, 1983), 2-3. |
| Collins, Brother | 1 | "Early Scenes in Church History," *Eighth Book of the Faith Promoting Series* (Salt Lake City: Juvenile Instructor Office, 1882), 30-31. |
| Free, Andrew | 14 | Edward W. Tullidge, *The Women of Mormondom* (New York, 1877), 157-58. |
| Hale, Sol | 17 | Professor J. H. Paul, "Don't Lie to an Indian," *Improvement Era* 33 (February 1930): 261-65. |
| Hamblin, Jacob | 13 | James A. Little, *Jacob Hamblin, Fifth Book of the Faith-Promoting Series* (Salt Lake City: Juvenile Instructor Office, 1881), 112-18, 131. |
| Hanks, Ephraim | 7 | Soloman F. Kimball, "Belated Emigrants of 1856," Part 1, *Improvement Era* 17 (1914): 290-94. |
| | | Stella Jaques Bell, *Life History and Writing of John Jacques* (Rexburg, Idaho: Ricks College Press, 1978), 168. |
| | | Mary Goble Pay, "Autobiographical Sketch 1843-1913," MS 11650 (Salt Lake City: LDS Church Archives), 5. |

| | | |
|---|---|---|
| Hendricks, Drusilla | 22 | Drusilla Dorris Hendricks, 1810-1881, "Reminiscences [ca. 1877]," MS-8299 (Salt Lake City: LDS Church Archives), 11-15. |
| | | *Henry Hendricks Genealogy,* 1730- (Salt Lake City: Woodruff Printing and Litho; LDS Church Archives), 19-23. |
| Horsley, Sister | 5 | William Horsley, "A Sketch of My Experience," *Juvenile Instructor* 28 (Salt Lake City: George Q. Cannon Publishers, 1893), 421-23. |
| Knight, Lydia | 23 | *First Book of Noble Women's Lives Series* (Salt Lake City: Juvenile Instructor Office, 1883), 43-49, 54-57. |
| Leonard, Abigail | 21 | Edward W. Tullidge, *The Women of Mormondom* (New York, 1877), 164-67. |
| Norris, Joel | 6 | Leon Hartshorn, *Inspirational Missionary Stories* (Salt Lake City: Deseret Book, 1976), 43-44. |
| Patten, David W. | 18 | Lycurgus A. Wilson, *Life of David W. Patten, The First Apostolic Martyr* (Salt Lake City: Deseret News, 1904), 43-44, 69-70. |
| Peterson, Marn | 20 | Myrtle Wilcox Kennington, *Treasures of Pioneer History, vol. 5,* comp. Kate B. Carter (Salt Lake City: Daughters Of Utah Pioneers, 1956), 221-22. |
| Phelps, Laura | 19 | Zula Rich Cole, *Valiant Hearts with Undaunted Faith and Devotion* (Salt Lake City: LDS Church Archives, Utah), 8-19. |
| | | Joseph Smith, *History of the Church of Jesus Christ of* |

| | | |
|---|---|---|
| | | *Latter-day Saints, Period 1, History of Joseph Smith the Prophet, Vol. IV* (Salt Lake City: Church of Jesus Christ of Latter-day Saints, Utah). |
| | | Parley P. Pratt, ed., *Autobiography of Parley P. Pratt* (Salt Lake City: Deseret Book, Utah, 1938), 180, 215, 217, 221, 224-25. |
| Rich, Sarah | 24 | Sarah DeArmon Pea Rich, *"Autobiography 1885-1893,"* MS-1543 1-3 (Salt Lake City: LDS Church Archives, Utah), 22, 24-25, 27. |
| | | Edward W. Tullidge, *The Women of Mormondom* (New York, 1877). |
| Rollins, Mary | 16 | Elsie E. Turley Barrett, *"Mary Elizabeth Lightner,"* MS-3538 (Salt Lake City: LDS Church Archives, Utah), 6-8. |
| Smith, Amanda | 12 | Edward W. Tullidge, *The Women of Mormondom* (New York, 1877), 122-23, 128-31. |
| | | *Heroines of Mormondom, Second Book of Noble Women's Lives Series* (Salt Lake City: Juvenile Instructor Office, 1884), 87-92. |
| Smith, Andrew | 11 | Solomon F. Kimball, "The Hero of Linister," *Improvement Era* (January 1913): 207-8. |
| Smith, Joseph F. | 8 | Joseph Fielding Smith, comp., *Life Of Joseph Smith* (Salt Lake City: Deseret News Press, 1938), 136. |
| | | *Heroines of Mormondom, Second Book of Noble Women's Lives Series* (Salt Lake City: Juvenile Instructor Office, 1884), 20. |

| | | |
|---|---|---|
| Smith, Samuel H. | 9 | Lucy Mack Smith, "History of Joseph Smith," *Improvement Era* (1902). |
| | | *Times & Seasons,* vol. 5, no. 14 (August 1, 1844). |
| | | Dean Jarman, *The Life and Contributions of Samuel Harrison Smith,* a thesis submitted to the College of Religious Instruction, Brigham Young University (Salt Lake City: LDS Church Archives, 1961). |
| Snyder, Jane | 3 | Jane Snyder Richards, "Autobiographical Sketch 1881 Mar. 30–31," MS-11741 (Salt Lake City: LDS Church Archives), 2–3. |
| | | Jane Snyder Richards, "Collection 1837–1961," MS-1215, Box 13 fds 4–8, Reel 15 (Salt Lake City: LDS Church Archives), 2. |
| Taylor, John | 15 | B. H. Roberts, *Life of John Taylor* (George Q. Cannon & Sons Co., 1892), 134–50. |
| Unwavering Convert | 2 | Melvin S. Tagg, *The Life of Edward James Wood, Church Patriot,* a masters thesis presented to the College of Religious Instruction at Brigham Young University, 1959, 39–41. |
| Wallace, Melford | 10 | Albert P. Wallace, "Preaching The Gospel in Kentucky," quoted in N. B. Lundwall, *Faith Like the Ancients, vol. 1* (Paragon Printing Co., 1950), 292–95. |

# Index

## About the Author

Marlene Bateman Sullivan was born and raised in Sandy, Utah. She attended Dixie College, the University of Utah, and Utah State University. In June 1974 she married Kelly R. Sullivan, and the two have seven children. As a free-lance writer, Marlene has published articles and stories in numerous newspapers and magazines.

## Do you know an LDS Hero or Heroine?

Do you have a courageous ancestor, a fearless aunt, a noteworthy neighbor, or a faithful friend? Submit your story for consideration to be in our next volume of *Latter-day Saint Heroes and Heroines.* Stories should be no longer than 2000 words, and stories about living persons (if they are selected) will require a written release from that person before they are printed. No stories will be returned. Please include SASE for response and mail your heroic stories to

Heroes and Heroines
Aspen Books
2961 West California Avenue Suite E
Salt Lake City, UT 84104